PRAISE F(

MW01265234

The Ethan Gage Napoleonic Adventure Series:

NAPOLEON'S PYRAMIDS: "Dietrich is becoming a leader among historical novelists."
—Library Journal

THE ROSETTA KEY: "The action in nearly nonstop, the humor is plentiful, and the intrigue is more than enough to keep the pages turning."
—School Library Journal

THE DAKOTA CIPHER: "Fast, fun and fill of surprises . . . rich in intrigue and impressive historical detail."
—Publishers Weekly

THE BARBARY PIRATES: "An action-filled romp that's both historically accurate and great fun."
—Library Journal

THE EMERALD STORM: "A breathlessly exciting adventure."
—Booklist

THE BARBED CROWN: "Description of war on the high seas is rarely better than in this novel."
—San Antonio Express-News

THE THREE EMPERORS: "An especially interesting underlying tension of mysticism and science."
—Historical Novel Review

And For Dietrich's Nonfiction:

THE FINAL FOREST: "Engrossing and well-written, this is a model of balanced reporting and reasoned analysis."

—Publishers Weekly

NORTHWEST PASSAGE: "A marvel of history, nature writing, politics and common sense, extensively researched, lovingly written, and splendidly woven together in an epic story of a magnificent river and humanity's conquest of nature."

—Los Angeles Times

NATURAL GRACE: "Dietrich's colorful writing makes each subject come alive, leaving the reader with a newfound appreciation for the most basic elements of life."

—E Magazine

THE NORTH CASCADES: "A soul-stirring story of the history and challenges facing the rugged North Cascades."

—Signpost, Washington Trails Association

NAPOLEON'S RULES:

LIFE AND CAREER LESSONS FROM BONAPARTE

ALSO BY WILLIAM DIETRICH

NONFICTION

The North Cascades
Green Fire
On Puget Sound
Natural Grace
Northwest Passage
The Final Forest

FICTION

The Murder of Adam and Eve
The Three Emperors
The Barbed Crown
The Emerald Storm
Blood of the Reich
The Barbary Pirates
The Dakota Cipher
The Rosetta Key
Napoleon's Pyramids
The Scourge of God
Hadrian's Wall
Dark Winter
Getting Back
Ice Reich

NAPOLEON'S RULES:

LIFE AND CAREER LESSONS
FROM BONAPARTE

WILLIAM DIETRICH

March, 2015
ISBN 978-0-9906621-5-0
Burrows Publishing
www.williamdietrich.com

Book Cover Design/Interior Design by VMC Art & Design

He who fears being conquered
is sure of defeat.
Napoleon Bonaparte

TABLE OF CONTENTS

INTRODUCTION
THE FIRST MODERN MAN

D o you want to conquer the world?
Or just understand yourself?
Napoleon Bonaparte can help.

He was not only one of the greatest success stories of world history, but also one of its spectacular failures. He died a prisoner in exile on a lonely island in the South Atlantic at the age of fifty-one, comparing himself to the mythical Prometheus, chained to a rock.

Winner. Loser. Ruler. Exile.

We can learn from a guy like that.

Napoleon was soldier, emperor, invader, liberator, tyrant, reformer, builder, destroyer, revolutionary, reactionary, leader, manipulator, looter, giver, husband, adulterer, charmer, and bogeyman. An English nursery rhyme warned that Bonaparte would eat naughty children.

Oh my.

In France, Napoleon embodied national glory. He carefully cultivated his own image, was self-satisfied enough to give copious advice, and made pronouncements for posterity. Bonaparte was obsessed with his place in history, and his maxims are as prolific as the commonsense homilies of Benjamin Franklin.

Napoleon's statements are more debatable than Old Ben's, however, because he teaches from failure as well as success. Because of that, Bonaparte is particularly instructive. The self-crowned emperor is the general who gambled it all away in Russia. The conqueror of Europe could never get at Britain across the English Channel. The soldier who enthralled his troops was a brooder, confessing to few friends and no love. He was triumphant, but dissatisfied. A Colossus, but cornered.

"What a novel my life has been!" he exclaimed in exile on St. Helena.

Israeli military historian Martin Van Creveld called him, "the most competent human being who ever lived," in his book, *Command in War*. French historian and statesman Gabriel Hanotaux credited him with "the richest natural gifts ever received by mortal man." His foreign minister Charles Maurice de Talleyrand-Périgord said in retrospect, "His career is the most extraordinary that has occurred in one thousand years . . . He was clearly the most extraordinary man I ever saw."

(Napoleon called Talleyrand, "shit in silk stockings" after one of the minister's periodic betrayals.)

Bonaparte has plenty of detractors. Some historians have made careers critiquing almost everything Napoleon did, including his morality, personal conduct, strategy, tactics, diplomacy, code of laws, and civil administration. Historian

Owen Connelly's military biography of Bonaparte is titled *Blundering to Glory.*

"History is written by the winners," Bonaparte said. Unfortunately for him, he ultimately lost. He had a dizzying ascent from artillery captain in 1793 to emperor of France and master of most of Europe by 1807. Then he fell into unending war in Spain, a disastrous invasion of Russia, abdication, exile, and final defeat at the Battle of Waterloo in 1815. Napoleon had divorced Josephine for a loveless political second marriage in order to father an heir, was excommunicated by the Pope, and had some of his closest advisors turn on him.

From such heights, and depths, we learn. How could a Nobody from an impoverished, backward island in the Mediterranean – Corsica – go so far in his adopted France? And how could this Somebody, with an empire that stretched from Madrid to Warsaw, and from Hamburg to Naples, fall so fast and so completely?

The truly noble figures of history, such as Saint Francis of Assisi, Abraham Lincoln, or Gandhi, are easy to admire and difficult to emulate. They seem a step above, and a step removed. Not Napoleon. He was brilliant but flawed, lucky and unlucky, hailed and betrayed, revered and friendless. He was a genius so painfully human that in his life we find examples of the best and worst in our own.

This book grew out of research for my Ethan Gage series of adventure thrillers, featuring an American rascal and Franklin protégé who struggles to survive in Napoleon's tumultuous world. Ethan has a wry view of the greats with whom he mingles, and describes a brilliant yet very fallible Bonaparte.

What a time the pair inhabit! The late eighteenth and early

nineteenth centuries spawned the political, scientific, and industrial revolutions that produced our modern world. The era's strivers and eccentrics lived life as grand opera. Battle still had glory. Ships still had beauty. Dresses were scandalous, generals were peacocks, palaces were as grand as they were drafty, and furnishings had over-the-top ornateness. All was perilous risk and outrageous reward, with scant security and wild opportunity. Ethan and his wife Astiza are my novels' central characters, but Napoleon is the blazing sun around which all the historical figures revolve. Few men have so dominated their era.

Napoleon's contradictions seem modern, the stuff of gossip magazines, reality show confessionals, and TV psychiatry. Hitler, Stalin and Mao were so horribly warped that they are evil enigmas. Genghis Khan and Attila are far removed in mind and environment. Caesar, Hannibal, and Alexander are ancient. Napoleon opponents Wellington and Kutuzov were military men answering to political masters.

Bonaparte was both master and commander, ruler and instrument, who won his own battles. He endured the fame and scrutiny given modern politicians. He started from nothing, once so impoverished that he had to pawn his watch to buy a uniform coat. He was a climber, a self-promoter, and an opportunist. He seems embarrassingly recognizable in our twenty-first century – the self-made man, the entrepreneur, the egotist, the scrambler, the poser, the wit – and thus understandable, if not entirely understood by himself.

Certainly he loved to talk about himself. His contemporaries added far more. By an estimate of Encyclopedia Britannica, there are two hundred thousand books about Napoleon Bonaparte. French historians double that total, according to the International Napoleonic Society. More than any person in history!

This Napoleon book is about *you.*

This is not just a collection of Napoleon's maxims. Nor is it a complete biography, although its pages give a guide to Napoleon's career. It is a book to consider your own life and career through the lens of quotations and episodes that portray Napoleon's thoughts, successes, and failures. He instructs and bewilders. I cheerfully plunder his trajectory to glean practical lessons for business executives, entrepreneurs, military officers, cubicle captives, students, or anyone else who is ambitious and wondering what to make of life.

Napoleon is also fun. As a novelist, I declare that no fiction writer would dare create such an improbable figure, because no reader would swallow it. Only the historical fact of his existence makes Napoleon's story believable.

Which is why it is interesting to hear what Bonaparte has to say.

Chapters are organized by advice the general and emperor might give, taken from his own statements and examples. Bear in mind that debate continues over whether Napoleon was good or bad, visionary or narcissistic. The Dutch author Pieter Geyl published a historical compendium of opposing views called *Napoleon, For and Against,* in 1949. Nothing has been settled since. All we can do is apply our critical thinking skills.

While this book frequently quotes Bonaparte, historians sometimes extract the maxims from their broader context. Additionally, there were no digital recorders in Napoleon's day, so many of his attributed words are what others tell us he said.

We can imagine the emperor commenting, "Yes, but,"

or, "Did I really say that?" For example, "An army marches on its stomach," is often attributed to Napoleon. But it may also originate with Frederick the Great, and doesn't appear in English until the twentieth century. It possibly was not uttered by anyone famous at all. Attributing pithy wit to The Great is one way to make it go viral.

That doesn't make the idea untrue. The maxim makes a good point – that armies rely on food and logistics – and Napoleon would probably be happy to take credit for it, since he did for so much else.

Besides, history is a very imperfect story. Or, as Napoleon commented, "What is history but a fable agreed on?"

Even fables can be instructive.

To quote Napoleon again, "The only author who deserves to be read is he who never attempts to direct the opinion of the reader."

This is typical Bonaparte, contradictory to other statements he made and hypocritical in the extreme, since he can be said to have invented modern censorship and propaganda. Napoleon wrote to direct opinion all the time, most famously in his Army Bulletins that exaggerated victory and minimized defeat. If any giant of history tried to influence readers' opinion it was Napoleon, down to his St. Helena memoirs and dying day.

No matter. His argument was that authors should let facts speak for themselves.

So consider the facts and words, and come to your own conclusions.

RULE 1
STAND FOR SOMETHING

Napoleon's enemies accused him of seeking nothing but world domination and self-aggrandizement. We all know the caricature: short, feisty, power-mad, and impatient. A me-me-me kind of guy.

There's some truth to that. (Though his height was quite average for France at the time, as we'll see.)

Yet that summary by the hostile (think England) is not how overachiever Bonaparte saw himself. Ambitious? You bet. A glory hound? Yes, he fed on fame. Power hungry? "Power is my mistress. I have worked too hard at her conquest to allow anyone to take her away from me."

But he also believed he was fighting not just for himself, or even for France, but for the ideals of the French Revolution. "A revolution is an idea which has found its bayonets," he said. "I am the Revolution."

What did this mean? The revolutionary ideas Napoleon

adopted and enforced included an end to feudalism, promotion by merit instead of birth, secular schools, religious tolerance, equality before the law, property rights, honest and efficient administration, and patronage of science and the arts.

Bonaparte believed his bayonets thrust reform home, and that there was thus a method to his militarism. His conquest of kings meant liberation for the masses, he claimed. He was no George Washington, since the American refused kingship and voluntarily retired from presidential office. But Napoleon kept a bust of Washington in his Tuileries palace, and when the American died in 1799 the First Consul ordered ten days of mourning.

And because Bonaparte stood for something, people stood with him.

Napoleon was born into a world of huge income inequality, the haves and have-nots determined by the lottery of birth. His wars partly overthrew that, allowing ordinary people to change their station in life. Many of his generals rose from the ranks. Of his twenty-six marshals, or top commanders, Lannes and Mortier were sons of farmers, Ney the son of a barrel cooper, Lefebvre the son of a miller, Oudinot the son of a brewer, Masséna the son of a tanner, Murat the son of an innkeeper, and Suchet the son of a silk maker. Bessières started as a barber.

Napoleon encouraged this. He expanded French education, taking it out of the hands of the church and making schooling widely available. He boosted middle class standards of living. He created a new Legion of Honor determined by merit. His dream of what he would leave behind was not entirely dissimilar to today's European Union, with a single currency, porous borders, unity, and opportunity – but with him and his heirs in charge.

"It is not against me, exactly, that the powers make war," Napoleon justified. "It is against the (French) Revolution. They have never seen in me anything but the representative, the man, of the Revolution."

Or, at another point: "If we have battled in every part of the Continent, it is because two opposing social orders were facing each other."

A critic can complain that this is the justification of a warmonger. Shortly before his final battle at Waterloo, Napoleon confessed, "I wanted to rule the world, and in order to do this I needed unlimited power. I wanted to rule the world – and who wouldn't have in my place? The world begged me to govern it."

Actually, much of the world begged him to go away.

Yet in his lust there is that special word, "govern." Napoleon truly thought of himself, with considerable justification, as an organizer and reformer, not just a conqueror and tyrant. In a Europe rusty with feudalism, aristocracy, moribund economies, and even the Inquisition in Spain and Italy, he brought the shock of the new.

Dreams of European unity dated back to memories of the fallen Roman Empire and rulers such as Charlemagne. Napoleon updated it. "Europe is but one province of the world," he said. "When we make war, we make civil war."

So he would wage the wars to end all wars, by putting everything under French domination. He dreamed of making Paris, "capital of the world."

"There must be a superior power," he argued, "which

dominates all the other powers with enough authority to force them to live in harmony with each other – and France is best placed for that purpose."

How much was idealism, and how much was megalomania?

There is no question that the revolutionary armies that arose in the 1790s were defending and exporting revolutionary ideas that came out of the Enlightenment and the American and French revolutions. Equality, fraternity and liberty threatened the old order, and the deposing and massacre of aristocrats was a direct threat to the European establishment that lorded it over the masses.

Much of the world lived in slavery or near-slavery in 1800: black and Indian slaves in the Americas, slaves in the Islamic world, serfs in Russia and Eastern Europe, and land-bound peasants in China and India. Poverty was extreme. Rank was frozen.

So the struggle was in part about money – who could seize it and who could keep it. Bonaparte's upheavals made him a bizarre, inadvertent sort of Robin Hood, plundering the foreign rich, sharing the spoils with his followers, and raising the French and European middle class with political reform, public works, trade, and promotion. (Not to mention thirty-nine palaces for himself, some of which he never got around to visiting.)

He also organized France and his Empire with an efficiency and tyranny not seen since ancient Rome, with all the good and bad that implies.

His Louisiana sale doubled the size of the infant United States, and his conquest of Spain made possible the revolutionary liberation of Latin America. He put in motion political tides that would unify Germany and Italy, reform Switzerland, set the stage for Norwegian independence from Denmark, and reignite the dream of Polish independence.

Napoleon's first advice would thus be to believe in something, if you want people to believe in you. What are you ultimately trying to achieve?

Not that he was consistent. Bonaparte struggled his whole life between idealism and personal ambition. Once power became its own excuse, he began to lose it. In the words of his liberal contemporary critic Madame Germaine de Staël, "He wanted to put his gigantic self in the place of mankind."

And so many of the people who once followed began to oppose.

He could not entirely win over his own family. Napoleon fell out with his younger brother Lucien, who accused him putting personal ambition before political principle. "I believe that a man should place himself above circumstances and commit himself to a definite choice if he wants to be something and to make a name for himself," Lucien wrote to his sibling Joseph. "The most hated men in history are those who sail according to the wind . . . I have always been aware of a completely selfish ambition in Napoleon."

But early on, Napoleon opened Jewish ghettos. He made civil law consistent and fair. Beethoven and Goethe lauded him, before changing their mind.

Individuals and organizations tend to make existence its own justification, and some businesses defend cancerous competition as natural capitalistic law that requires no excuse. Winning is better than losing, growth is better than stagnation, longevity is better than extinction, yada, yada, yada.

Napoleon made no such claims. In the end, he said, a leader has to justify his ambition by creating a greater good. "I love power," he admitted. "But it is as an artist that I love it. I love it as a musician loves his violin; to draw out its sounds and chords and harmonies." His music was progress.

He started his own *Arc de Triomphe* (the monument would not be completed for decades) but this was an exception to his rule. "Dedicating monuments to those who have rendered themselves useful to the nation is honorable to all nations – but it should be left to after ages to construct them, when the good opinion conceived of the heroes is confirmed." In his case, it largely didn't happen. While Paris has two hundred streets, places, or monuments dedicated to people, battles, or incidents of his reign, no street or monument is named for Bonaparte himself. There are only one or two statues to the man in the capital. He was, and is, too controversial.

Still, his lesson is to let those who come after you determine your worth, not the toadies seeking favor now. And ultimately, that worth will be measured by a cause deeper and broader than your own personal success.

RULE 2
PERSEVERE

"**I**f courage is the first characteristic of the soldier, perseverance is the second," Napoleon said.

The general practiced what he preached. His own greatest comeback came forty years after he was dead.

Following his final defeat at Waterloo in 1815, Bonaparte was exiled to the bleak South Atlantic isle of St. Helena, where he died six years later on May 5, 1821. King Louis XVIII (brother of the Louis XVI who had been beheaded in the French Revolution) had resumed the throne after Napoleon's exile, and had no desire to have the deceased conqueror bring his inflated reputation back to France. So Bonaparte was buried with an unmarked headstone under a willow tree in the Valley of Geraniums. The man who had dominated Europe for nearly two decades was tucked away about as far as it was possible to be. Good riddance, establishment Europe said.

Then politics swirled. Times changed. Memories softened.

In a political gamble the Président du Conseil to new king Louis Philippe, Adolphe Thiers, suggested in 1840 that Napoleon's return to France could help reconcile French opinion about a tumultuous past that included the French Revolution, Napoleon's empire, and the royalist restoration. By this time "Boney" was old news, so Britain had no objection. A French ship was sent to St. Helena to bring back the body.

Like a Russian babushka doll, Napoleon had been laid to rest in a tin coffin, inside a mahogany one, inside a lead coffin, and inside another mahogany one. When all this was pried into, French and British officials found a remarkably preserved body still dressed in Napoleon's favorite green uniform of a colonel of the *chasseurs,* or light infantry. Cancer had thinned his corpulence. The skin was waxy pale.

After brief examination the body was repackaged, this time in six successive coffins that in aggregate weighed a ton and a half. (The idea was preservation, not that the corpse was some kind of vampire who must be sealed away.)

Napoleon had asked to be buried near the banks of the Seine amid the French people. After careful consideration authorities chose Les Invalides, a church and military hospital located at what were then the outskirts of Paris. One advantage was that the tomb site was fenced and could be locked against rallies and demonstrations.

Napoleon's tomb thus went from one extreme, obscurity, to the other, monumental. Three-quarters of a million people turned out for his funeral procession. It took sixteen black horses to tow the heavy death assemblage under the new *Arc de Triomphe.* A winter sun shone, as it had at his imperial coronation and the victory at Austerlitz decades before. While spectators were subdued, some of the iconography of the procession used Christ-like symbolism of sacrifice and resurrection. There were even rumors (which have never completely died) that Napoleon's tomb had in fact been found empty, and that the Corsican adventurer had somehow escaped confinement.

Napoleon was interred in the Chapel of Saint-Jerome at the Invalides while his permanent resting place was designed for the adjacent Dome Church. Architectural competition resulted in a design being chosen in 1842, but construction wasn't completed until 1861. Four decades after his death, Napoleon's multiple coffins were finally placed inside a sarcophagus of red quartzite on a green granite base. The tomb is surrounded by twelve marble "Victories" celebrating Bonaparte's most famous battles, and ten bas-reliefs celebrating his domestic achievements.

These are: pacification of France, centralized administration, a State Council, his Civil Code, his Concordat bringing back the Catholic Church from its revolutionary exile, Imperial University, court of accounts, code of commerce, public works, and creation of the Legion of Honor.

The dazzling domed space includes the tombs of brothers Joseph and Jerome, four famous generals, and Napoleon's only son, Napoleon II, who his father styled "King of Rome." After Bonaparte's fall the younger Napoleon was brought to his mother's Austrian home and died in that country in relative obscurity, of tuberculosis at age twenty-one. Bizarrely, it was Adolf Hitler who transferred those remains back to Paris, after Hitler conquered France. He sent them as a good will gesture to the Nazi-allied Vichy government.

And so Bonaparte rests, in swankiness somewhere

between the glory of St. Peter's and the gloss of Las Vegas. Napoleon must be smiling inside all those coffins. So what if his wars killed several million people? He yearned for glory and got his monument, four decades after his death.

He who rests in the best tomb wins.

Bonaparte's life had at least five other remarkable comebacks. Napoleon was a master of the ability to persevere, snatching victory (or at least survival) from the jaws of defeat. He was a wily opportunist who worked from whatever circumstance he found, until fortune turned his way. Give him lemons, and he made lemonade.

His life was a rocket. He was sent from his native Corsica (an Italian-speaking island off the coast of Italy) to boarding school in France when he was nine. His ne'er-do-well, spendthrift attorney father died when he was fourteen. As the self-appointed head of his family, Bonaparte completed a difficult two-year artillery course in a year, was a French army lieutenant at age sixteen, a brigadier general at twenty-four, conqueror of Egypt at twenty-eight, First Consul (or military dictator) of France at thirty, Emperor at thirty-five, defeated at Waterloo at forty-five, and dead at fifty-one.

The official cause of death was cancer, which killed his father. Theories have persisted that he was either intentionally poisoned by the British or inadvertently poisoned by environmental contaminants such as rat poison. Another idea is that poorly prescribed medicines combined in his stomach to become toxic.

How did he soar? He kept at it, believing that when one door closes, another opens. "People have many projects in life but little determination," he said.

Some of his famous comebacks:

Bonaparte had dreamed of liberating and ruling his native island. But in June of 1793, he and his family were forced to flee his native Corsica after running afoul of a dominant faction led by local patriot Pasquale Paoli.

Solution to exile? Carve out a bigger career in Napoleon's newly adopted France. One step was the respelling of his name from the Italian Napoleone di Buonoparte to Napoleon Bonaparte.

Another bounce back came after the 1793 siege of Toulon, when Napoleon's rapid military rise became imperiled. His patron Augustin Robespierre fell from power with his more powerful brother Maximilian after the two fostered the Reign of Terror. Both were executed in 1794. Bonaparte had become entangled in France's cutthroat revolutionary politics and was identified with the losing side. He found himself under house arrest for two weeks.

Solution? An impassioned letter protesting his innocence to key political deputies, coupled with a reminder of his victory at Toulon. He was already too damn good not to employ.

Perform, plea, petition. The government swiftly put him back to work.

Napoleon found himself in peril again in 1799 after conquering Egypt for France. British Admiral Horatio Nelson cut the young general off from reinforcements by destroying the French Mediterranean fleet at the Battle of the Nile. Soon after, Napoleon was defeated at the siege of Acre, in present-day Israel. His strategic position was doomed. It was the end of Bonaparte's fantasy of Asian empire, and the wayward adventure should have been the end of his career.

Solution? Abandon his army. (He informed his successor general by letter, rather than face-to-face.) He sailed away to France ahead of the bad news, avoiding British naval vessels on the way, played the hero at home, ignored suggestions from enemies that he be tried for desertion, and seized absolute power in a coup d'état.

When Napoleon's initial clumsy demand for power was met with angry rejection by inflamed legislators, he gathered some troops, ordered them to invade the chamber with bayonet, and sent the deputies fleeing out the windows. If at first you don't succeed . . .

Middle East loser? No way. He was "the sword" France was looking for. It had been a calculated risk. While on his way to mount his coup, he passed the plaza where the guillotine had been used to execute thousands during the Reign of Terror. He remarked that he would shortly either sleep in the Luxembourg Palace or have an appointment with that same guillotine.

He slept in the palace.

Once he was military dictator, Napoleon's rise was astonishing. Within five years he had crowned himself emperor and in ten had conquered most of Europe. Yet all seemed lost after his disastrous defeat in Russia in 1812, where an army of more than six hundred thousand men dissolved to nothing from battle casualties, disease, cold, and desertion.

"He that makes war without many mistakes has not made war very long," Bonaparte observed.

Once more, Napoleon was finished. Or was he?

He left the last survivors, rushed to Paris before opposition could be organized, and raised a new army of conscripts that would fight to keep him in power until the allies forced his abdication in 1814. This stand cost another half-million men, but it illustrates Napoleon's tenacity.

And that was it.

Except it wasn't.

Napoleon was exiled to the island of Elba, not far from his native Corsica, and given a miniscule guard and court. Surely he was finished! But no, he escaped Elba under the nose of British warships, landed in France ruled by the hapless Louis XVIII, seized power a second time, and mustered an army to defeat his enemies piecemeal in Belgium. This famous comeback attempt has come to be known as The Hundred Days.

He almost pulled it off before being defeated at Waterloo. "The nearest run thing you ever saw in your life," said the victor, the British Duke of Wellington. The battle left about fifty thousand dead and wounded on the two sides.

And finally Boney *was* finished, exiled to a rock in the South Atlantic.

Until he was brought back to the most glorious tomb in Paris, and perhaps the world.

The point here is not that Napoleon was ultimately defeated. We all are by firings, illness, accident, layoffs, forced retirements, bad investments, divorce, social upheaval, and death.

"To have a right estimate of a man's character," Napoleon said, "we must see him in misfortune."

In misfortune, Bonaparte wouldn't give up.

Let's not go overboard with praise of the doughty Corsican. Napoleon was endlessly confident because he had more than his share of success. He was born into minor Corsican nobility (his family applied for, and got, recognition as one of seventy-eight noble families on the island) and he received an excellent French military education. His abilities were recognized early, he found powerful patrons, he remarked frequently on his good luck, and his setbacks were always from higher and higher positions of power. He was resilient, but only after a track record of incredible achievement.

But his determination to master circumstances, instead of being bound by them, marked him apart from his rivals. He hung in there.

There are other historical examples.

George Washington lost more battles than he won in the Revolutionary War, but he succeeded with persistence. So did Ho Chi Minh and General Giap in Vietnam.

Ulysses S. Grant resigned as captain in the peacetime army, failed at farming, failed at business, and drank too much. But he became the Civil War's most successful general, was twice elected president of the United States, and, when afflicted with throat cancer, wrote a memoir that became the biggest bestseller of its time.

Abraham Lincoln lost when he ran for reelection to Congress, lost twice when he ran for the Senate, and failed to become a vice-presidential candidate. But he did become America's greatest president.

Franklin Delano Roosevelt's political career looked over after losing a run for vice president in 1920 and being crippled by polio in 1921. Yet he worked furiously to regain some mobility, rose to the White House in 1932, and was elected to four terms.

Nelson Mandela served twenty-seven years in prison for protesting Apartheid, but became president of South Africa. Then he was forgiving about the whole thing.

Mahatma Gandhi and Martin Luther King were also repeatedly jailed.

Winston Churchill seemed politically finished by the 1930s. But he came out of political exile to lead Great Britain to victory in World War II. His party lost power again in 1945, but bounced back so that Churchill could serve as prime minister again from 1951 to 1955. He had bulldog tenacity.

Perseverance has been key in business, entertainment, sports, and the arts. Steve Jobs was fired by Apple, and came back to make the computer company the biggest corporation in the world in stock value.

Soichiro Honda was turned down by Toyota for an engineering position so he went off and started Honda Motors.

Harry Potter was rejected by a dozen publishers, and *Gone With the Wind* by thirty-eight. In fact, scores of books that eventually became famous bestsellers were turned down by scores of editors. Author Jack London collected six hundred rejections – and then wrote fifty books in fifteen years, becoming the most popular American writer of his time.

Vincent Van Gogh sold only one of his nine hundred paintings in his lifetime, and bad luck and mental illness caused him to take his own life. But his work today is valued collectively at well over a billion dollars.

Auguste Rodin was rejected three times by the prestigious École des Beaux-Arts in Paris – and went on to become the best-known sculptor in France.

Walt Disney was fired by a newspaper editor at his first job because he "lacked imagination and good ideas."

Oprah Winfrey was fired from her first television anchor job and told she wasn't fit for TV.

Thomas Edison was pulled out of school by his parents after teachers called him "stupid" and "un-teachable." He later said the invention of a commercial light bulb required persistent trying of six thousand different kinds of filaments: six thousand failures that led to one great success.

Albert Einstein didn't speak until age three, was considered lazy by his teachers, and was rejected for university teaching positions. He had to take a job in the Swiss patent office. There he remade our concept of the universe.

Charles Darwin was judged "rather below the common standard of intellect" as a child. It took him three decades of thinking, observation, and writing to formulate the theory of evolution.

Julius Caesar wept that he hadn't accomplished anything by thirty-three, the age at which Alexander the Great had died.

They all kept going.

So did Napoleon, stumbling often and recovering all the same.

"Victory belongs to the most persevering," he said.

RULE 3
DEFINE YOURSELF

N apoleon was so successful, and so famous, that in popular imagination he became a caricature of himself. That bicorn hat turned sideways, the plain gray greatcoat, and the hand in his waistcoat (a common mannerism in portraits of the time) were recognized by followers, parodied by English enemies, mimicked by madmen, and turned into countless cartoons.

His pose was on purpose. To rule and command, Bonaparte needed to be recognized. First he defined himself. Then he created his image.

He worked on being a celebrity.

Actors have struggled to get inside Napoleon because *he* was an actor, playing to the masses like any politician. The thespian temptation is to make him stiff and remote, a forbidding statue. In fact, Bonaparte was restless, charismatic, anxious, sensual, bullying, a showboat, and capable of calculated rages to achieve an effect. His life is so jam-packed with adventure that it has defeated attempts to summarize it in movies. Silent film director Abel Gance wanted a multi-part film, but never got past the first one. Director Stanley Kubrick had to give up his own plans for a Napoleon biopic because of lack of financing for such a sprawling biography.

It takes a cast of millions.

No matter. In the author's opinion, dramas that get close to the truth of Napoleon are *The Godfather* and *The Sopranos*. The don't know when to stop pathos of the chemistry teacher turned drug lord in *Breaking Bad* would qualify too. Bonaparte was like a Mafia don, the slum kid who builds a violent empire and earns the enmity of the establishment. Bonaparte was Italian by birth and culture, and biographers have compared him to renaissance intriguer Cesare Borgia or the Borgia admirer, author Niccolò Machiavelli. Napoleon's family, marshals, and hangers-on were his gang. In ancient Rome, the titles were patron (patronus) and client (clientele).

But how to win over the world?

Long before others defined Napoleon, he invented himself. He didn't allow others to pigeonhole or limit him. He never asked permission. He never waited his turn. He didn't worry about what he must do or should do to conform to his rank and responsibilities at any particular time. He imagined what he *could* do.

The Corsican Napoleone di Buonaparte, distantly descended of Tuscan nobility in Italy, was a pugnacious, brilliant, dreamy, climber. The typical image of him in plump, self-satisfied middle age forgets the lean, eagle-nosed, longhaired military firebrand who became the rock star of the French Revolution. He promised his public that he could pluck order out of chaos, refining the tumult of liberty and equality into something sustainable and coherent. He was not content to play the subordinate. He wanted to command. He *had* to command. And he didn't always wait for life to turn his way.

"Circumstances? What are circumstances? I make circumstances," he declared.

Not that he was ever consistent on this point. Napoleon regularly contradicted himself about the interplay of free will and destiny and so he also said, "As a rule it is circumstances that make men." He was acutely aware of how the opportunities and accidents of history had accelerated his rise, and how the same accidents could bring him down.

"I have made all the calculations; fate will do the rest."

He viewed life as a ticking clock, giving himself a good decade of rule to accomplish what he wanted. The forecast was remarkably prescient.

This dance between circumstance and will, between origins and ambition, and between destiny and choice, fascinated the Corsican. Sometimes he regarded himself as protected by fate: "The bullet that will kill me has not yet been cast."

At others he proclaimed himself in command of it. "Imagination governs the world!"

He imagined his future empire and a peculiar kind of afterlife of historical glory, not in heaven but here on earth. Napoleon expressed few thoughts on the afterlife, but he talked constantly of his desire to be remembered.

"Glory is fleeting," he said, "but obscurity is forever."

What set him apart were furious ambition and the

determination to rise by both opportunity and shrewd, ruthless maneuver.

He also achieved power through calculated charm. He had the knack of directly engaging people with his gaze, be it common soldier, mistress, or Tsar Alexander I. He could flatter by listening and making perceptive comments that cut to the heart of an issue. "Do not blush to ask questions," he advised his stepson Eugene. "Know how to listen, and be sure that silence often produces the same effect as does knowledge." Napoleon was confident enough in his intellect that he encouraged debate and discussion.

Those who served him often adored him. "The nearer you viewed him, the greater he appeared," said his Palace Prefect, Baron Louis de Bausset-Roquefort.

Napoleon also cultivated his image as hero to an initially enthused public. He seemed the ultimate self-made man, the exemplar of merit over birth. And for a long time he was a winner, exciting France with victory the way a successful football coach or winning quarterback excites people today. His fans shared his glory. Early on he could win a decisive battle like Marengo in Italy at the cost of a thousand dead and 3,600 wounded. Triumph was relatively cheap. Nine years later, public opinion was turning by the time of his "victory" at Wagram, when French casualties were a bloody 34,000. The battles of Borodino and Leipzig were even worse.

But early successes gave him enormous self-confidence and political popularity. His victory at the battle of Lodi in Italy, in 1796, was a relatively minor affair in a long campaign, but he came away with startling ambition. "That evening, for the first time, I no longer considered myself a mere general," he wrote in his memoirs, "but a man called upon to decide the fate of peoples." He was twenty-six years old, with a ragtag and outnumbered army. But he'd already come so far! Isolated in military school for his accent and poverty, the young general was showing them all.

This confidence eventually evolved into pride, which contributed to his downfall. A more modest man would not have gambled all by invading Russia.

But neither would he have accumulated the means to do so.

Napoleon was born August 15, 1769, as the second of eight surviving children. His rambunctious, curious, aggressive personality earned him the nickname "Rabulione," or, "He who meddles in everything."

His family was minor Corsican nobility: upper middle class in status, we might say today, though his substantial house was rustic by French standards. His attorney father's decision to work with French occupiers helped win the nine-year-old Napoleon a place in French military academies. Napoleon's aptitude for war appeared early. The children were given a playroom they could alter for their games, including drawing on the walls. Napoleon drew rows of soldiers.

He dominated his older brother Giuseppe, or Joseph. Psychologist Sigmund Freud theorized that Napoleon was driven by sibling rivalry. The two brothers later actually became close when Joseph was a subordinate ally, but then distant again when Joseph bungled the throne of Spain that his brother had given him. Napoleon also alternated between promoting and quarreling with brothers Louis, Lucien, and Jerome.

Bonaparte had mother issues. Letizia, a compact Corsican beauty, was pious, strong-willed, uneducated, and ambitious for her children. She also had crafty common sense. She hoarded most of the income of a million francs a year that her famous son eventually gave her. When asked why, she replied, "Who knows, one day I may have to find bread for all these kings I've borne." She outlived Napoleon by fifteen years, dying in Rome at eighty-five.

Napoleon's quick mind and aptitude for mathematics and history were recognized by French teachers, but he was a loner with an Italian accent and limited social skills. (The Italian that set him apart in school in France proved a valuable asset in his first big command in Italy, where he used the language to pump local officials for information.)

At school, Napoleon was so surprised by ice, which he had never seen in Corsica, that he accused classmates of putting glass in his water basin. This resulted in merciless teasing, of course. The foreigner was poor, hopeless at music and dance, clumsy with girls, a brooder, and a loner. He grew up with a chip on his shoulder.

Given his gloom (and one wonders if he was mildly bipolar), Napoleon had an adolescent flirtation with suicide. "Always alone in the midst of men," he wrote at sixteen, "I come to my room to dream by myself to abandon myself to my melancholy in all its sharpness. In which direction does it lead today? Toward death. What fury drives me to my own destruction? Since die I must, is it not just as well to kill myself? Since nothing is pleasure to me, why should I bear days that nothing turns to profit? Life is a burden because I taste no pleasure; all is pain."

Like many teens, his ambitions were unfocused. He wrote short stories and a novel, read about great generals, and pushed to graduate quickly when his father died, since he felt responsibility for his family.

He didn't know where he was going. But he did know that he had to master circumstance.

Fortunately for Napoleon, along came the tumult of the French Revolution in 1789, just as he was turning twenty. "Revolutions are good times for soldiers of talent and courage," he later remarked.

Napoleon had been commissioned a second lieutenant four years before and assigned to routine garrison duty with a French artillery regiment. He was not one to attend to dull duty while awaiting events. He wrangled nearly two years of leave from the lackadaisical royal army and spent much of that in Paris and Corsica, scheming, drifting, attending to family issues, and striving to win a leading role in a Corsican independence movement opposed to French rule.

The French Revolution initially seemed to provide opportunity for Corsican freedom. By 1793, however, that possibility was fading and Napoleon had run afoul of the complex shoals of island politics between royalists, republicans, and Corsican nationalists. He and his family were forced to flee to the French mainland.

His self-invention as would-be island revolutionary was over.

So he started anew. At age twenty-four he won appointment to command of artillery at the siege of Toulon, where French revolutionaries were besieging royalists and their British allies. Napoleon sized up the situation, criticized his superior until he got a new one, skillfully dominated the harbor with his guns, forced the British to evacuate, took a blade wound in the thigh in courageous hand-to-hand combat, and was promoted to brigadier general.

If he could not free his native Corsica, he would become the greatest general in his adopted country. He redefined himself.

After the brief house arrest mentioned in the proceeding chapter when Robespierre fell, Bonaparte was reinstated in the army while becoming engaged to Eugénie Désirée Clary of Marseilles. (She is best known to history as Désirée, but Napoleon called her Eugénie.) Then he got a new assignment.

Which Napoleon refused.

France was less united than it is now – a third of its twenty-eight million didn't even speak French – and the French government wanted its newly minted general to take an infantry command against French rebels in the Vendée, an Atlantic coast region south of Brittany. Bonaparte considered the infantry a step down from the artillery, and thought a guerilla war against provincial French rebels and royalists sounded like a career dead end.

In punishment for balking, Napoleon was removed from the general's list in regular service and was briefly on half pay with few prospects. He toyed with additional reinventions, even asking to be transferred to Constantinople to offer his services to the Ottoman Sultan. He wrote a bad romantic novella called *Clisson and Eugenie,* a thinly disguised idealistic portrait of his own romance. He prowled Paris, looking for patrons. His quick rise seemed stymied.

Then came violent opportunity.

When conservatives fomented a Paris rebellion against the ruling National Convention, Directory leader Paul Barras turned to Napoleon to crush the threat.

The assignment meant firing on Frenchmen, but this time Bonaparte didn't hesitate. The Vendée was a quagmire, but here in Paris was crisis that could make a career.

Napoleon sent a young cavalry officer named Joachim Murat galloping across Paris to seize some cannon. (Murat would later become a marshal and brother-in-law, marrying Napoleon's sister Caroline.) Then our man of the hour, who had criticized timid King Louis XVI for not fighting back against revolutionary mobs, used his guns to mow down several hundred Parisian rebels.

Revolt smashed. Problem solved. Image recast. Bonaparte was the tough guy, the enforcer, "the sword" the revolutionary government needed.

As a reward, Napoleon was given command of the Army of Italy. He was only twenty-six years old.

Barras was also looking for someone to take a mistress off his hands. The politician had become bored with the widow Josephine de Beauharnais, a Creole from Martinique with two children. Her husband had been beheaded in the Terror, and Josephine had come close to sharing the same fate.

Marriage in those days was as much calculation as romance. The thirty-two-year-old Josephine recognized Bonaparte, six years younger than herself, as a comer. Napoleon saw a still-sexy widow with the social skills he lacked. He was smitten, Josephine was desperate, Désirée was dumped, and the marriage documents were doctored to make man and wife both twenty-eight.

(Interestingly, Désirée may have gotten the best of the bargain. Her sister Julie married Napoleon's brother Joseph, and Désirée married a French marshal, Jean Bernadotte. This marshal was invited to become Crown Prince of Sweden when that country was trying to placate Napoleon's empire. Eventually Bernadotte turned on Napoleon, the Corsican fell, and the French pair became Sweden's king and queen three years after Bonaparte's final exile. They founded a dynasty that continues to this day.)

Josephine, meanwhile, was divorced by Napoleon in 1809 for failing to bear him a son. She died of pneumonia in 1814, shortly after his first abdication.

The lesson is that a setback, like a broken engagement, may turn out for the best. And a triumph, like winning a husband from a rival, may prove a bitter victory.

Be careful what you wish for. And be cautious what you rue.

All this was in the future. In 1796-97, young Napoleon not only won a brilliant campaign in Italy, he exceeded his authority to negotiate a favorable peace. He boldly cultivated military celebrity in France. He wasn't just heroic, he promoted his reputation as hero with a fine instinct for propaganda.

Then came another assignment he didn't like: invade England.

Time to take charge of his future again.

After deciding an invasion of Britain was impractical because of English sea power, Napoleon instead resuscitated a long-standing idea to invade Egypt, a semi-independent appendage of the Ottoman Empire. The French hoped they could use Egypt as a base to contest British domination of India and the Indian Ocean.

When Napoleon's victorious Egyptian army subsequently became marooned by Nelson's victory at the Battle of the Nile, Bonaparte simply ran home and seized power in Paris.

He drafted a new constitution making himself military dictator, and in 1804 held a plebiscite to legitimize his ascension to emperor. The doctored vote was three million in favor versus 1,562 opposed, with brother Lucien inventing at least half the votes supposedly cast.

Through all this, Bonaparte never waited patiently for promotion or permission. He sought powerful patrons until he could safely dispense with them. He made himself ruler of Egypt, and emperor of France. He grew rich, and shared riches to buy loyalty. He ignored complaints that he was presumptuous and self-serving. Over the course of a decade – from his graduation from military school until his first big victories in his mid-20s – ordinary Napoleon decided to be extraordinary.

"The reason most people fail instead of succeed is they trade what they want most for what they want at the moment," he once said. Bonaparte played a long game. His eye was for bigger and bigger prizes.

To summarize some principles Napoleon operated under:

- **Work for Yourself.** Bonaparte took long leaves, avoided or refused assignments not to personal advantage, and fought to get top command as early as possible. He made France's victories his own. His competence helped make this self-aggrandizement possible.

- **Cultivate Patrons.** When it was to his advantage, Bonaparte worked with Pasquale Paoli to try to control Corsica. He courted Terror leaders Augustin Robespierre and fellow Corsican Antoine Christophe Saliceti to rise in the revolutionary army. He schmoozed Directory member Paul Barras to negotiate the shoals of Paris politics, and built a cabal of men including his brother Lucien, speaker of the French Assembly, to pull off a coup. He used allies and then rose above them. "If I want a man," he said with his soldiers' earthiness, "I am prepared to kiss his ass."

- **Marry well.** Josephine had little money, but she had a sophisticated understanding of Parisian social life that Napoleon lacked. Marrying her would make her former lover Barras a patron who could grant an army. She had glamour, Napoleon had power. But when she couldn't give Napoleon a son, he divorced her (apparently with real regret, Josephine screaming in despair) and married Archduchess Marie Louise of Austria in an attempt to unify his European holdings. This wife *did* produce a son, but she deserted Napoleon for her one-eyed lover Adam Adalbert, Count von Neipperg, after Bonaparte's first abdication in 1814.

- **Don't Accept Thankless Assignments.** Napoleon saw no advancement in boring garrison duty when he might dabble in politics in Corsica, no glory in a difficult campaign against French rebels in the Vendée, and no chance of successfully invading England in 1797. He didn't want a superior's gratitude for following orders. He wanted the kind of flashy success he garnered in Italy and Egypt, so he could seize power and become the boss. "I can no longer obey," he said, "I have tasted command and I cannot give it up."

Admirable? Not in polite society.

Liked? "Friendship is only a word. I care for nobody."

Patient? Napoleon could wait for opportunity, but not for anyone else. He made a lot of enemies and created a lot of jealousy, and eventually it caught up with him. But we don't much remember his rivals. We remember Bonaparte.

Who defined who he was, and what he would become.

"A throne is only a bench covered with velvet," he said. "I am the state."

No one ever accused him of false modesty.

RULE 4
PROMOTE YOURSELF

A movie star is more than a good actor. He or she has magnetism, a presence on the screen that goes beyond beauty or deep-voiced stage authority. Sometimes their life becomes part of their performance. Their command of attention is hard to explain or teach, but utterly seductive.

Napoleon had that gift. He wasn't just the smartest guy in the room, he filled the room, wooed the room, cowed the room. Some contemporaries described him as mesmerizing and some as fearsome – one woman said he had the eyes and manner of someone you would dread meeting in a dark alley – but all attested to his star quality. Without royal blood or great wealth, he dominated with personality.

The awkward youth became, by conscious will, the commanding man.

Napoleon's presence developed over time, and may never

have matched that of today's superstars who have the constant feedback of the camera. But British opponent the Duke
of Wellington said his presence on the battlefield was worth
forty thousand men, in both skill and inspiration.

Bonaparte started quite ordinary. He was not tall, but
not dramatically short, either. The British estimate that he
was five foot two was the result of substituting English inches
for French ones. Napoleon was more accurately a shade over
five-six in American inches, the average male height for the
time. The term *petit corporal* that he won in Italy was one of
affection by his troops instead of descriptive; Napoleon was
never a corporal and "petit" in French is sometimes used to
refer to a romantic partner.

But neither was he tall, and he is repeatedly described as
alarmingly thin when young, even "hollow chested." His skin
had an odd yellow tone, as if he had jaundice. In his teens he
was so gangly that female acquaintance Laure Permon teased
that he looked like "Puss & Boots," with sword and boots
too big for him. Like all slights, it was one he never entirely
forgot. His oddly cut hair fell raggedly and greasily to his
shoulders, and he was not graceful. Despite his love of music,
he sang out of tune.

Contemporaries report Napoleon did have a pleasing
speaking voice, good teeth, and arresting gray eyes. If not movie star handsome, he commanded attention with a sharp nose,
piercing gaze, an amused mouth, and a share of wit and humor.
When a cannonball whizzed over the scalp of a nearby officer,
he quipped, "It's a good thing you're not any taller!"

Like many young men he grew into his body in his
twenties, the hero on horseback. But he could not rely on

looks; he needed presence. This developed with success and confidence.

Napoleon was physically courageous. By his own calculation he fought in sixty battles, losing only seven. Scholar Gunther Rothenberg counted thirty-four major clashes in his *The Napoleonic Wars*, of which Bonaparte lost six. Napoleon was seriously wounded by a pike or bayonet at Toulon, was hit in the boot by a spent bullet at the battle of Aspern-Essling, and had his boot clipped by a cannon ball in 1814. He was thrown from horses, had mounts shot out from under him, nearly drowned at Boulogne, and campaigned despite nagging ailments and disease. At the battle of Arcole in Italy, he rallied his men by waving a flag until other officers dragged him to safety. At Lodi he personally aimed cannon. His soldiers knew this and respected him for it. He was a combat commander, and it gave him the aura of command.

So did his costumes. "A king," Napoleon said, "does not exist in nature, he exists only in civilization; there cannot be a naked king – he is only a king when he is dressed." So he dressed for distinction.

While he wore robes costing in excess of one hundred thousand francs for his coronation, his preferred business clothes were white waistcoat covered with the green coat of a colonel of the *chasseurs* or the blue coat of the *grenadiers*. It was a reminder that he was a soldier first, the source of his power. He wore no braid or medals. This simplicity wasn't modesty. It made him stand out amid the peacock splendor of courtiers and fellow officers.

His famous felt hat with simple tricolor cockade was made more distinctive by being worn sideways to accentuate his shoulders. It became such a trademark that even when not wearing it he would carry it around by the brim, as a mark of identity.

Others have copied this strategy. Abraham Lincoln used his stovepipe hat to emphasize his height and stand out in a crowd. Authors Mark Twain and Tom Wolfe distinguished themselves with ice-cream-white suits. Apple's Steve Jobs went for a black mock turtleneck and jeans. Singer Johnny Cash became "The Man in Black." Einstein is remembered for unkempt white hair, and Dolly Parton and Cher for their wigs and figures. Facebook's Mark Zuckerberg has adopted gray T-shirts as daily wear. Gangsters affect suits, oilmen cowboy boots, priests clerical collars.

"A general must be a charlatan," Napoleon said.

He invented and mastered modern propaganda, using frequent publications to promote himself at a time of rising public literacy. After seizing power in 1799, he was supposed to rule as one of three "consuls" who would share power. But the day after the coup, Paris was plastered with posters emphasizing Napoleon's role while entirely omitting mention of his two partners, Abbé Emmanuel Sieyès and Pierre Roger Ducos. It was part of his swift campaign to seize command by making himself the sole object of public adulation.

(Just in case his rivals missed the point, Bonaparte set his own initial salary at half a million francs a year and theirs at 150,000 each.)

He began referring to himself by his first name in the fashion of monarchs, and made his initial, 'N,' a decorative element in Paris.

Napoleon paid particular attention to the opinion of

soldiers. He used his phenomenal memory to greet some by name and deed, and shared their hardships without stooping to be too familiar. He believed leaders must keep a calibrated distance to retain discipline and an aura of mystery. But he recommended military reviews lasting as long as eight hours so that commanders could personally eye and inspect every member of their ranks. The attention made the men feel special.

Given that Bonaparte couldn't shout to the entire army, he wrote to it with printed "Orders of the Day."

"It is not that addresses at the opening of a battle makes soldiers brave," he explained. "The old veterans scarcely hear them, and recruits forget them at the first boom of the cannon. Their usefulness lies in their effect on the course of the campaign, in neutralizing rumors and false reports, in maintaining a good spirit in the camp, and in furnishing matter for campfire talk. The printed order of the day should fulfill these different ends."

For civilians, he issued Bulletins for consumption back in France, editing events to excite his followers and sustain morale. They so minimized French losses, and so exaggerated those of the enemy, that "to lie like a Bulletin" became a cynical army phrase. But early on they inspired the general population.

In 1797 he started a *Journal of Napoleon* to promote his own image, and over the course of his generalship and rule he struck 141 different commemorative medals to celebrate his victories and achievements.

Since Napoleon seized power instead of being born to it, he invented spin control. "Four hostile newspapers are more to be feared than a thousand bayonets," he said, and so he shuttered sixty out of the seventy-three newspapers in Paris. He established and controlled six others. He censored plays and books. He exiled intellectuals who were overly critical, ordering Madame Germaine de Staël not to reside within forty leagues (120 miles) of Paris.

He stamped his symbol, the industrious bee, everywhere he could. He consciously made these trademarks as ubiquitous as the former *fleur-de-lis* of French royalty, thus anticipating the corporate logos of today.

Napoleon contended such self-promotion was necessary. "There is a great deal of difference between free discussion in a country whose institutions are long established and the opposition in a country that is still unsettled," he argued. France was tumultuous, torn between royalists, moderates, and radicals. Bonaparte would be the glue to hold them together.

While Napoleon managed to assert control over opinion in France during his reign, foreign newspapers attacked and ridiculed him. Assassins plotted to kill him. Domestic rivals circled like sharks when he began to lose. Everyone weighed in with memoirs when it was all over, many of them critical. Bonaparte conducted a struggle for public opinion that lasted his entire life and beyond. It continues unabated to this day.

He looted Italy and Egypt of art and sent it to Paris, identifying himself as an arts patron by stocking the Louvre, which he renamed *Musée Napoleon*. Even on campaign he wrote to admonish officials who had shortened Louvre visiting hours, believing the stolen art was tangible evidence of the benefits of his rule. He befriended and supported artists such as Jacques-Louis David and Antoine-Jean Gros, whose paintings inflated his legend the way a favorable television commercial would today.

Both men romanticized their historic paintings. David, for example, painted Napoleon astride a rearing white stallion as he crossed the 8,100-foot-high Great St. Bernard Pass of the Alps in his 1800 Italian campaign. The truth is that the conqueror rode up one side of the mountains on a sure-footed mule, and slid partway down the snow on the other side on his bottom.

Gros painted Napoleon leading a charge across an Italian bridge at Arcole, but in reality he briefly rallied troops on a dike nearby. Gros also famously showed the general comforting French soldiers who were plague victims in the Holy Land. His visit was indeed risky in an era when transmission of plague was a mystery, but the painting was designed to counter reports that Napoleon gave hopeless victims opium for euthanasia, rather than evacuate them from pursuing Turks. (He did lend his horse to a wounded soldier.)

The ruler didn't stop at paintings to enhance his image. Monarchs had always used pomp and ceremony to solidify their reign, and Napoleon loved military reviews and parades. In the era before television, this was how a militarized society shared experience. Cannons boomed in Paris. Bands played martial music. Half a million French came for Napoleon's coronation as emperor in 1804, and twenty thousand of the elite crammed into the actual ceremony inside Notre Dame. Napoleon consciously put on a show.

His coronation ceremony was as carefully choreographed as the Academy Awards or a royal wedding, down to dressing up the cathedral façade and insisting that his sisters carry

Josephine's train. His surprise crowning of his own head and that of his wife in front of the startled audience was calculated to make him the talk of Europe.

Public sentiment and support, he said, were the foundation of political power. "The moral is to the physical as three to one," he said, referring to both military morale and public approval.

He created a Legion of Honor to recognize and enlist soldiers and civilians of use to the state. One ceremony was held on a bluff above the English Channel (a body of water called *La Manche*, or The Sleeve, by the French) and involved crashing cannon, crashing bands, crashing surf, and a crushingly long line of decoration recipients in sight of the England they hoped to eventually invade.

"What is the government? Nothing, unless supported by opinion," Napoleon said.

And, he advised, "Men who have changed the world never achieved their success by winning the chief citizens to their side, but always by stirring the masses."

This is routine calculation today, but a new idea in Bonaparte's time.

He also knew such opinion was ephemeral. "The people scarcely know what they desire," he warned. Solution? "Public opinion is ever on the side of the strongest."

Napoleon was not just an actor, of course. He knew his long-term success depended on military victory, able civil administration, and public works. He had to accomplish. He had to win.

"The indestructible pages of great reigns are the battles and the gigantic works. It is there where historians must find their materials."

It's not the title on the door, or the office in the corner, it's the confidence and partnership of the people you lead.

"Power is founded on opinion," Napoleon said.

RULE 5
BE LUCKY

"**I** know he is a good general, but is he lucky?" Napoleon reportedly once asked of a promising subordinate.

He meant the question quite literally. Napoleon was levelheaded, but he had a strong superstitious streak common to his native Corsica. He would pick out his "star of destiny" in the night sky and point it out to others. (Be careful about these stars. Another who thought he had one was General Custer.)

Napoleon's "luck" was his courage to seize opportunity from circumstance. He was lucky that favorable winds enabled his escape from Egypt to France in 1799, lucky that good weather accompanied his Alpine crossing in the 1800 Italian campaign, and lucky that direct hits exploded enemy ammunition wagons in the battles of Rivoli and Marengo, helping turned the tide in his favor. But all this luck required boldness, and boldness carried risk.

He was unlucky that winds and fog allowed his siege artillery to sail into British hands before the 1799 battle of Acre, unlucky that winter came early in Russia in 1812, and unlucky that rain soaked the Waterloo battlefield in 1815 and delayed his attack, giving the Prussians time to come to the aid of Britain's Duke of Wellington.

Napoleon was never entirely consistent in his views on fate and free will, asserting at one moment that he made his own luck and the next that he was a creature of fortune with a dictated destiny.

"All that is to happen is written down," he said. "Our hour is marked, and we cannot prolong it a minute longer than fate has predestined."

Yet he also said, while exiled on St. Helena, "Great men are rarely known to fail in their most perilous enterprises. Is it because they are lucky that they become great? No, but being great, they have been able to master luck."

By which Napoleon meant his extraordinary ability to take advantage of rapidly changing events and personalities.

Biographer Frank McLynn wrote that because Napoleon "saw his life as a novel, nothing in it surprised him." As a result, he had the audacity to lead an adventurous expedition to Egypt, seize power, crown himself emperor, and reorder Europe as the chance arose.

Historians and psychologists have speculated that Napoleon in a sense lived a dual life, the "real" Bonaparte observing the deeds of the celebrity Napoleon. "I had risen from the masses so suddenly," he later wrote. "I felt my isolation. So I kept throwing anchors for my salvation into the depths of the sea."

And, "It is said that I am ambitious, but this is an error; or at least my ambition is so intimately allied to my whole being that it cannot be separated from it." Napoleon could not help being Napoleon.

One of Bonaparte's great mistakes — and great advantages — was his lack of a master life plan beyond the desire to achieve and rise. This hampered the strategic hard choices and compromises needed to sustain his empire. His extreme competitiveness and unwillingness to give up gains made him lose perspective. But he wasted very little time chasing unobtainable goals. His tendency to improvise also made him flexible.

His dream of carving out an empire in Asia was blithely abandoned after his defeat in the Holy Land in 1799.

He dreamed of empire in North America but gave up on that after his intended occupying army was wiped out by yellow fever and slave revolt in Haiti. Instead, he sold the Louisiana Territory to the United States in 1803.

He created empire in Europe because, well, one thing led to another.

He was the ultimate opportunist, building on his victories and moving past defeats. He wanted greatness and glory, but weaved his way toward them like a running back dodging tacklers in a football game.

Adolf Hitler was so bound to his racial theories and German expansion to the east that he invaded the Soviet Union when it made little military sense, since Britain remained undefeated. Napoleon invaded Russia with no theory at all, plunging into war out of pride, frustration that Tsar Alexander was ignoring his dictates, and the vague instinct that Russia was the next place to conquer — as if that might somehow solve his problems.

Both invasions were disasters, but one came from fanatic ideology, and the other from an ill-focused need for control and earnest belief in luck. Yes, Napoleon had his reasons – humble the Czar, bring Russia into the embargo against England, push on toward Asia – but there is a curious fatalism to Napoleon's career. What was his goal? To go as far as he could. What were his means? Destiny. What could go wrong? Fate.

Thus Napoleon's question was not unreasonable. "Is he lucky?"

The Roman senator Seneca defined luck as preparation meeting opportunity. Under this definition, Napoleon excelled.

"Ability is of little account without opportunity," the Corsican said.

An example was how he won his first artillery command at the siege of Toulon. Bonaparte prepared by being an unusually able artillery officer and tactician. He had long practiced writing, and thus attracted revolutionary attention with his literary flair for political propaganda. He also prepared by studying fortifications in his native town of Ajaccio, recognizing that the lines in Toulon were similar. Result: "luck."

When a Paris mob threatened the shaky Revolutionary government, Bonaparte's hardheaded observations of out-of-control riots at the Tuileries and Toulon had convinced him the best response was ruthless repression, or what writer Thomas Carlyle called "a whiff of grapeshot." The way to deal with a mob was to mow it down. Yes, he was lucky in being in the right place at the right time. But he made his own luck with careful observation, pitiless judgment, and preparation. He seized the needed cannons before the mob could.

"All great events hang by a single thread," Napoleon said. "The clever man takes advantage of everything, neglects nothing that may give him some added opportunity; the less clever man, by neglecting one thing, sometimes misses everything." Napoleon was meticulous.

If his strategic thinking to create a permanent European empire was sometimes muddy, his tactical planning for a particular campaign, battle, or political event involved months of careful thinking. "Genius is an infinite capacity for taking pains," he said. "We must take things as we find them, and not as we wish them to be . . . Great men are those who subdue both bad luck and fortune."

He was so successful that he was sometimes *too* improvisational. His logistical preparation for the Egyptian expedition was faulty. The boats he built in hopes of crossing the English Channel were not seaworthy. His army in Russia quickly outmarched its supplies.

He would lurch from one project to the next, repair a risky venture with a brilliant comeback, alienate an ally and charm an enemy, and thus didn't have the ordinary necessity to come to grips with himself and his own limitations. He always thought he could out-think and out-work any obstacle. Of course, he succeeded in doing so for nearly two decades – but a more prudent man might have built a smaller, more lasting empire.

Confidence is necessary. Cockiness is fatal.

Napoleon also lacked ordinary empathy. His callousness was useful to a general ordering troops to their death, but a severe handicap as a human being. He was not a psychopath – he could be generous, emotional, and even sentimental on occasion – but he had a heroic view of history in which he was at the center of events. To die in service for France and Napoleon Bonaparte could give life meaning, he advised his followers.

There was a Silicon Valley joke about billionaire entrepreneur Larry Ellison that went, "What is the difference between God and Larry Ellison? God doesn't think he's Larry Ellison." The same satire could be applied to Napoleon, one of history's great egotists. He used soldiers, women, and family. He so disliked losing that he would cheat to win at card games, and then pay back the loser his winnings.

He also had a sadistic streak, making a habit of pinching and striking members of both sexes who displeased him.

Napoleon believed in omens, portents such as comets, and lucky days. He deliberately sought battle at Austerlitz on the one-year anniversary of his coronation as emperor, and won his greatest victory there.

He disliked Fridays and the number thirteen.

He was a Deist, believing in a distant and impersonal God, but nonetheless crossed himself in the Catholic manner when excited. At the same time he despised organized religion and warred so often with the Pope that he was eventually excommunicated from the Church, on June 11, 1809. Napoleon's frustration with Rome had led him to annex the Papal States, the Pope excommunicated the French emperor, and Napoleon in turn arrested and exiled Pius VII.

The two eventually came to political conciliation out of self-interest in empire and church, but neither liked or admired the other.

Napoleon also seemed to genuinely believe that he was periodically visited by a gnome from French history called

"The Little Red Man." This creature had the power to fore-tell the future. Some historians regard Bonaparte's claim of the encounters as fiction, and others theorize that he hallucinated them under stress. Real or not, The Little Red Man reinforced Napoleon's sense of himself as a plaything of fate.

So he was superstitious.

He hated cats, believing them bad luck.

He was alarmed when pictures of Josephine broke because he considered her good luck. He later lamented that his decline in power and health occurred after he divorced her in 1809.

The result was a curious combination of fatalism and will. "Events carry with them an invincible power," he explained. "The unwise destroy themselves in resistance. The skillful accept events, take strong hold of them, and direct them."

That was his philosophy in a nutshell.

"Lead the ideas of your time and they will accompany and support you," he taught. "Fall behind them and they drag you along with them. Oppose them and they will overwhelm you."

But he could not always heed his own teachings. He led the early revolutionary ideals of liberation and reform, but as his empire grew he became more reactionary and ruthless. His ambitions diverged from those of France. His wars became pointless.

And when that happened, he fell.

RULE 6
STAY HEALTHY

"The best cure for the body is a quiet mind," Napoleon said.

It would be difficult for a leader to more completely ignore his own advice.

Napoleon led a vigorous, exhausting, demanding physical existence, and as a result was hampered by major and minor illnesses most of his life. Bonaparte's mind was brilliant, but restless, moody, impatient, melancholy, competitive, and relentlessly ambitious.

"I was born and made for work," he boasted.

His killer schedule wore him down, many historians believe. Napoleon's military occupation forced him to travel long distances, be outside in all weather, and spend a lot of time in the saddle or in badly sprung coaches on miserable roads. He began to dramatically age and fatten at thirty -eight, and was so tired at the final battle of Waterloo, at forty-five, that he was absent from the battlefield at critical times.

Here we learn what *not* to do from Napoleon's example.

Poor health hampered his decision making for the last seven years of his reign. He became alternately hesitant and impulsive, and tormented by afflictions such as painful urination and hemorrhoids. Everyone has ailments, but Bonaparte's decline surprised contemporaries who had seen his vigor as a young man. Witnesses wrote of his rapid weight gain, shortness of breath, lethargy, lost agility, and pale complexion.

It does not appear that Napoleon's health problems were necessarily genetic. While his father died of stomach cancer at thirty-eight, his mother lived to eighty-five. His siblings' ages of death, in birth order, were: older brother Joseph seventy-six, Lucien sixty-five, Elisa forty-three (sudden illness), Louis sixty-seven, Pauline forty-four (cancer), Caroline fifty-seven, and Jerome, seventy-five. While average lifespan in Napoleon's era was only about forty years, because of childhood mortality and accidents, an upper-class adult had a good chance of living considerably longer. Benjamin Franklin lived to eighty-four, Thomas Jefferson to eighty-three, George Washington to sixty-seven, and Napoleon's foreign minister Talleyrand to eighty-four.

Napoleon prided himself on a killer schedule. His workday typically began at 6:00 a.m. at home or in the field, with a bolted breakfast and review of events and newspapers – in a hot bath, when possible. Then came dictated correspondence, meetings, or campaigning. He worked until late at night, with a brief break for supper. He usually ate rapidly, and seldom lingered at the table. He would retire at midnight or 1:00 a.m., sometimes wake in the middle of the night with an idea for dictation, and then go back to bed before rising at 6:00 to start the punishing regime again.

Modern researchers say adults need seven to nine hours sleep per night. Most historians estimate Napoleon got little more than half that, even with ten minute catnaps that he would take on horseback on in a carriage.

"I have never found the limit of my capacity for work," he proclaimed.

But his body found that limit.

Napoleon paced as he dictated, huddled near fires because of frequent chills, unconsciously twitched his right shoulder to the point his coat would begin to shift off his body, picked absently at his skin until it bled, massaged the old battle scar from Toulon, and had a frequent and nervous cough. His impatient manner extended into bed, where Josephine complained of premature ejaculation. He was reported to masturbate before battle to relieve tension.

None of this seemed to dim Napoleon's extraordinary mind. He thought with unusual clarity in a linear, mathematical pattern, had a phenomenal memory for numbers and statistics, could recall faces with astonishing accuracy, and would sometimes awaken with intuitive thoughts produced by his subconscious. One minister recalled being asked by Napoleon about his daughters when the general had met them only once, for an instant, a decade before.

The workaholic operated in difficult environments. Napoleon campaigned in the broiling Egyptian desert and in freezing Russian snow. He crossed the Alps with his army. He conducted a siege in the Holy Land. He fought in Spain and Italy. He watched Moscow burn. He was thrown from horses, dunked in cold water, and had near misses from cannonballs and bullets. He endured rain, heat, insects, mud, and distance.

The modern road mileage from Paris to Moscow is 1,769. It probably exceeded two thousand miles on the meandering routes of Napoleon's day. This is shorter than the 3,700 miles of the Lewis and Clark Trail from St. Louis to the Pacific Ocean, but in his lifetime Napoleon probably easily accumulated as many miles, in his zigzags across Europe from Berlin to Madrid, as the American explorers. In a crisis, he could travel seventy-five to one hundred miles a day in a coach. Sometimes he slept in palaces and sometimes in a campaign tent. His portable iron bed, preserved in a Paris museum, looks considerably less comfortable than a modern air mattress.

Napoleon was described by those who knew him as thin, energetic and expressive when a young man. But he never had an athlete's vigor. He was "pale even to sallowness," said Englishwoman observer Fanny Burney, and many others commented on a yellow cast that turned with age to a disturbing marble white.

Some contemporaries described his light gray eyes as icy, and others as engaging. He had fine brown hair, small feet, and delicate hands he was proud of. He was as brusque to women as he was warm to his troops, but nonetheless managed twenty-one mistresses, by the count of biographer Andrew Roberts. He focused intently on whomever he talked to, a habit most found flattering, but a few considered disconcerting. He had at least one well-documented seizure – possibly epilepsy – after a tryst with an actress. He occasionally flew into rages.

He restricted himself to a cup or two of watered wine a day, and was never known to be drunk.

Observers noted his appearance began to dramatically change about 1807 or 1808. Napoleon himself remarked on the change. He gained weight, his head seemed to sink toward his shoulders, his hair receded, and his vigor declined. While captive on the British ship *Northumberland* after his defeat at Waterloo, he was described by Sir George Bingham as, "hair out of powder and rather greasy, his person corpulent, his neck short, and his *tout ensemble* not at all giving an idea that he had been so great or was so extraordinary a man."

In the eighteenth and nineteenth centuries, the greeting "How are you?" was not rote politeness. Medicine was primitive, sanitation poor, germs and antibiotics were unknown, and most diseases had yet to be properly identified, much less cured. Diets were monotonous, fresh fruits and vegetables were irregular, rooms were drafty and smoky, and tobacco and alcohol were abused. Even wealthy people were knocked out of commission for weeks or months at a time.

Napoleon was no exception. While his drinking was moderate, he inhaled snuff – tobacco – and paid little attention to diet or exercise. He occasionally hunted, but without great enthusiasm, and apparently was a poor shot. He hit his marshal André Masséna in a hunting accident – shades of American vice president Dick Cheney! – and reportedly needed seven shots to finish off a cornered stag.

Over the years he is recorded as suffering from fevers as a teen (possibly from malaria) and then, as an adult, from rashes, skin disease, headaches, constipation, chronic stomach pain, a concussion, seizures, severe difficulty urinating, severe hemorrhoids, and flatulence. He contracted scabies in Toulon in 1794, coughed blood in 1803, had a gastric attack at Bayonne in 1808, eczema in Vienna in 1809, a severe bladder infection at the Battle of Borodino in 1812, fever after a drenching at the Battle of Dresden in 1813, and exhaustion and crippling hemorrhoids at the final Battle of Waterloo in 1815.

Match all this with his early death on St. Helena, and experts have made a minor industry out of trying to diagnose the man. It didn't help that he despised doctors in general and his own physicians in particular. "Doctors will have more to answer for in the next world than we generals," he growled.

Speculative diagnoses, none confirmed, are malaria, liver disease, kidney disease, kidney stones, epilepsy, heart blockage (his pulse was recorded at a low forty beats a minute), venereal disease, schistosomiasis (infection with worms), nervous ischuria (difficulty urinating), neurodermatitis (skin scratching), and eczema, or skin irritation. And then cancer at the end, according to a British autopsy.

Napoleon's physical decline was matched by military and political decline. He began to fade as Spain rose in terrible revolt. He was sick for much of his invasion of Russia. He was exhausted, sleepy, and in pain at Waterloo. His military situation was still not entirely hopeless after the Waterloo battle – his enemies had suffered almost as many casualties – but he was uncharacteristically indecisive and spiritless. Bonaparte was finally worn out. Surely stress played a role.

His drive was admirable. But his brain put demands on his physique that it eventually couldn't sustain.

He was hardly unique in his health problems. Alexander the Great may have been an alcoholic. Julius Caesar had epilepsy. Abraham Lincoln suffered from crippling depression. Woodrow Wilson's stroke helped derail his hopes for reform after World War I. Franklin D. Roosevelt had polio. John F. Kennedy suffered from Addison's disease. Ernest Hemingway was bipolar, a common diagnosis among the highly successful. Tycoon Richard Branson of Virgin Airlines is one of more than a dozen famous CEOs diagnosed with dyslexia. Prime Minister Margaret Thatcher was one of countless leaders who battled insomnia. John D. Rockefeller lost all his body hair to alopecia.

Disease is as common among the powerful as it is in the general population. The American Center for Disease Control estimates half of all Americans has at least one chronic health problem, and the National Institute for Mental Health estimates one quarter have a significant mental health problem, such as depression, in any given year.

The lesson is that fame does not grant immunity. Don't let the goal of conquering the world conquer your body. Any successful individual eventually needs sufficient sleep, periodic rest, daily exercise, healthy eating habits, good hygiene, vacations, and, at times, counseling.

Even then they may struggle with serious disease. A career can be a balancing act between accomplishment and wellness.

Because some of Napoleon's last critical battles were so narrowly won or lost, it is intriguing to imagine history if Napoleon had been more of a health enthusiast.

Or took more naps.

RULE 7
BE CONFIDENT

D espite occasional setbacks, Napoleon enjoyed the advantage – and the handicap – of enormous self-confidence.

"In war," he once remarked, "you see your own troubles; those of the enemy you cannot see. You must show confidence."

He was bold in war, bold in politics, bold in reform, and bold in promoting his own image. He advocated taking action, speaking up, and being firm. "Ten people who speak make more noise than ten thousand who are silent," he said.

Vain? Ruthless? Annoying? At times. But he was entrepreneurial, and his success with armies made him a locker room leader, a super jock, the alpha male. Men followed him. Women submitted not necessarily to his charm, but to his corona of power. (There seems to be no evidence for later claims that he might have been bisexual, or that his sexual equipment was unusually small. His frequent romantic partners made no such observations.)

When Ulysses S. Grant took command of the oft-defeated Army of the Potomac in the American Civil War, its officers were obsessed with the wiliness of Confederate General Robert E. Lee. An impatient Grant told them to stop worrying about what Lee might do and start thinking about what the Army of the Potomac could do.

This kind of aggressive attitude comes from Napoleon's example.

"He who fears being conquered is sure of defeat," Bonaparte said.

He seemed born to rule. A story relates that when he was given command of the Army of Italy at age twenty-six, older officers were jealous of his political appointment. They refused the courtesy of removing their hats when meeting their general for the first time.

Napoleon sized up his subordinates with chilly gray eyes and briskly swept off his own hat. To not follow suit with a superior would be ridiculous, and so his officers had little choice but to copy. Then Napoleon jammed his own hat back on and told his new subordinates what he intended to do with their army.

"That little bugger really frightened me," veteran General Pierre Augereau remarked later.

Bonaparte was told before leaving Paris that at twenty-six he was too young to command the Army of Italy. He replied, "I will be old when I return."

Napoleon believed, above all else, in himself.

Four years before the Italian incident, and well before he

had accomplished anything of note, Bonaparte seemed to foresee a fiery future. "Men of genius are meteors destined to be
consumed in lighting up their century," he wrote at twenty-two.

Napoleon constantly preached command authority. "In-
decision in the leader engenders weakness and anarchy in the
results," he said, adding that, "Long councils of war result in
the adoption of the worst course, which is the most timid, or,
if you will, the most prudent," he said. "The only true wisdom
in a general is determined courage."

While opposing generals dithered, Napoleon always kept
his primary goal in mind, positioning his smaller army between enemy forces and defeating each enemy wing in turn.

He could also postpone immediate gains for greater ones.
To accumulate enough soldiers to meet an approaching Austrian army he quickly broke off the siege of Mantua, even
though it meant abandoning 179 siege cannon. Once he
defeated the Austrians in the field, Napoleon resumed the
siege, won the garrison's surrender, and recovered not only
those 179 cannon but 325 more.

Nor would he betray panic when things went poorly.
When Austrian forces got into the French army's rear before
the battle of Rivoli, Bonaparte's remark to his officers was,
"We have them now."

By the end of the one-year campaign and its furious
sequence of battles, his army of about forty thousand had
killed, wounded, or captured 120,000 Austrians.

How to explain Napoleon's extraordinary character? He
was clearly bright and pugnacious as a boy. His home island
was a rugged education: a poor, rustic, and violent backwater.
Bloody hanks of meat hung in the street market stalls, flies

buzzed off donkey manure, and offal stank. Death was routine: four of Letizia's twelve children died in infancy. It was an era in which there was no childhood as we know it. Children were miniature adults expected to work as soon as they were able. Sentiment was a luxury. Draft animals were machines and food animals were doomed to slaughter.

There was a strong Italian tradition of vendetta in Corsica. Jealousies were not just intense, but potentially deadly. Napoleon calculated that his maternal grandmother could call on three hundred relatives to come down from the hills in any dispute. He grew up in a Hatfield vs. McCoy culture. By French education he was an intellectual product of the Enlightenment, but his first years in Corsica were in a medieval milieu. In his hometown of Ajaccio, violence was the final arbiter of power, and money a key to survival.

When a teacher chose his brother Joseph to play a Roman and Napoleon a Carthaginian in a school play, Napoleon insisted the roles be reversed so he could be on the winning side.

The young Bonaparte's father Carlo was frequently absent and somewhat hapless. Napoleon never respected or mourned him. But his mother Letizia was ambitious for her children and a crafty disciplinarian. She knew her second son was a willful handful. He was apparently a habitual liar, an occasional petty thief, and had a child's cruelty: his mother was furious when Napoleon laughed at a crippled grandmother. When her son was eight and getting big for his tiny mother to catch and handle, she ambushed him. After he misbehaved as an altar boy she told him she wouldn't beat him, waited until he was changing his clothes and more vulnerable, pounced, and twisted his ear.

Napoleon took it as a useful lesson.

She also recruited Napoleon to spy when his father Carlo was drinking and gambling in local casinos, an assignment the boy hated.

Yet, "I owe her a great deal," he said later. "She instilled into me pride and taught me good sense." From his carefree father he may have inherited charm and magnetism, but from his stern mother he learned a habit of self-discipline and flinty shrewdness. He struggled to entirely satisfy her. She boycotted his coronation as emperor by staying in Rome, possibly because he had fallen out with his brother Lucien and possibly because she was feeling snubbed by his prosaic and very un-royal title for her of *Madame Mère,* or Madame Mother. They made up after he gave her a palace with two hundred servants and courtiers.

Napoleon later had her painted into David's famous coronation scene anyway, Letizia fictionally watching proudly as he crowned Josephine, a woman his mother despised. One wonders if her son meant her inclusion as a tribute or a rebuke.

At age nine, Napoleon was sent first to a school at Autun to learn basic French, and then to the Spartan military school of Brienne, run by monks, in the Champagne region east of Paris. It was a grim, mediocre institution with indifferent teachers, and Napoleon was poor at music, singing, dancing, and noble deportment. He did like military history, and was adept at mathematics. He always spoke French with an Italian accent.

Bonaparte did not make friends easily, was teased for his Corsican origins, and got into frequent fistfights. Each student was given a garden plot to tend, so Napoleon fenced his off and used it as a private refuge to read by himself.

The one moment his classmates remembered favorably was when he organized an epic snowball fight.

He came out of Brianne thin, tough, and determined when he went to the École Royale Militaire in Paris at age fourteen. This was a school for aristocrats and a considerable step up in luxury, but the price was academic rigor. Napoleon was again good at mathematics and history, and poor at languages, drawing, and dancing. One of his rivals was Louis de Phelipeaux , the two supposedly kicking each other under their desks. In the coming wars, Phelipeaux would remain a royalist and fight on the Ottoman-British side against Napoleon at the siege of Acre in 1799. The battle was one of Napoleon's first defeats, but his school competitor died defending the city.

As a student at the military institute, Bonaparte finished a two-year artillery course in one year. Getting a cannonball to fall in the right place required combining the gun's caliber and elevation with the weight of shot, amount of powder, and wind, and Napoleon excelled at such calculations. Only four students out of seventeen at his school subsequently passed the rigorous artillery exam. Napoleon was one of them, and was commissioned a second lieutenant at age sixteen.

This was still the old France, ruled by Louis XVI. The king's government had succeeded in helping the American colonies win independence, but the cost of the war had left crippling debt. France was bankrupt and tottering toward its own revolution. Army life was tedious, with officers often going on leave all winter when darkness and bad weather made campaigning difficult.

Napoleon was still a provincial kid, preoccupied with his

dream of independence for his native Corsica. There was no sign of future greatness. Part of his time in the army was spent trying to salvage rights to a mulberry orchard on Corsica that his father had invested in. He lost his virginity to a prostitute in Paris at age eighteen.

But when the French Revolution broke out, he rose quickly.

His unhappiness at school, the death of his father, defeat in the politics of Corsica, and nagging poverty had given him quiet desperation that sometimes leads to success. Napoleon was also a shrewd judge. He realized the adult world was full of nonentities, and that his intellect and energy were superior to many men his senior.

The French initially had two bickering and incompetent generals in command at his first big battle, the siege of Toulon. Napoleon ever afterward recognized the importance of unified command. "One bad general is worth two good ones," he would later remark. "Success depends upon unity of action."

In the ensuing twelve years, his deeds raised him from artillery captain to emperor. "Impossible is a word to be found only in the dictionary of fools."

He looked for confidence in the men who followed him. "It is the unconquerable soul of man, not the nature of the weapon he uses, that ensures victory," he declared.

And, "True character stands the test of emergencies."

Several of his victories were narrow ones, but Napoleon had the confidence to hold fast. "The first qualification for a general-in-chief is a cool head," he said. A more ordinary leader would have ordered retreat at the 1800 battle of Marengo, where the French were desperately outnumbered, but Napoleon calmly waited all day for the reinforcements that eventually came. Even after his 1812 catastrophe in Russia, he didn't despair or mourn. He hurried back to Paris to raise a new army.

He also learned that most people hesitate while he could act. "Nothing is more difficult, and thus more precious, than being able to decide."

Napoleon wasn't always right, but even when wrong he moved so quickly that it often didn't matter. "In order to smash it is necessary to act suddenly," he preached. He calibrated risk and reward the way he calibrated cannonball trajectories. "He who hazards nothing gains nothing."

And, like a chess player waiting for the right opening, or the poker player waiting for the right hand and key psychological moment, Napoleon was a master of timing. His favorite tactic was to feint, get the enemy to commit to an ill-considered counterattack, and then hit their flank or rear.

At the battle of Austerlitz he deliberately weakened his center to give the Russians and Austrians overconfidence. They weakened their own to send a crushing attack against Napoleon's right flank, just as he expected.

Bonaparte held his counterpunch out of sight in fog until midmorning, and then attacked heights he had evacuated just two days before. Surprise was total, the enemy was split, and the victory was so complete that it left Russian Czar Alexander weeping under a tree.

"In war there is but one favorable moment," Napoleon said. "The great art is to seize it."

That takes confidence.

RULE 8
BE PRAGMATIC

Napoleon could on occasion be impractical or stubborn. He persisted in trying to economically strangle Britain with Continental embargoes that hurt France more. He refused to extract his army from his miscalculated intervention in Spain, turning the Iberian Peninsula into a Napoleonic Vietnam that cost France more than a quarter-million men. He indulged a greedy Josephine and grasping relatives, was occasionally foolishly faithful to hangers-on he should have fired, and could never ignore a military challenge when it would have been wiser to seek peace.

And yet . . .

He was usually the most practical, hardheaded, and calculating of men, to the point of skepticism and even cynicism. He dealt with life as it was, rather than how he wished it to be.

To Napoleon, the buck stops here. "A commander cannot take as an excuse for his mistakes an order given by his sovereign when the person giving the order is absent from the field," he said. If you're the person in charge and the one on the scene, he explained to his marshals, then success or failure is yours, not some distant king's. That means no dreaming, no wishing, no hoping, and no blaming. Just bloody pragmatism.

Napoleon didn't usually cling to projects that failed. He later said the brief interlude in Egypt and the Holy Land were among the happiest days of his life, but once the expedition became untenable, he hurried back to Paris. Meanwhile, an Arab fanatic assassinated the unfortunate general appointed to take his place.

When Napoleon's hope of reestablishing a vibrant French empire in North America was dashed by the annihilation of his army in Haiti (killing the husband of his sister Pauline), he coolly sold Louisiana to the United States for $15 million, equivalent to $230 million in 2014 dollars. The cash would help fund his planned invasion of England. Interestingly, the U.S. borrowed money from English banks for the purchase, meaning Napoleon arguably used cash from Britain to buy arms to invade it. Bankers are pragmatic, too.

Napoleon needed financiers, but didn't like them any more than he liked priests or doctors. "When a government is dependent upon bankers for money, they and not the leaders of the government control the situation," he warned.

So he kept borrowing to a minimum. His budget relied on high taxes for a very pragmatic reason: France had lousy credit. Bonaparte was a fiscal conservative by necessity.

When his hopes of conquering Britain became impractical because of naval defeats that culminated in the Battle of Trafalgar in 1805, he quickly abandoned the invasion project to which he'd devoted the last three years. Instead, he marched his army from the Channel Coast to a showdown with Austria and Russia in central Europe. Practicality again, dictated by events and geography.

"It is only by prudence, wisdom, and dexterity that great ends are attained and obstacles overcome," the emperor said. "Without these qualities, nothing succeeds."

He applied his shrewdness to politics. "A leader is a dealer in hope," he said, anticipating the campaign slogans of Bill Clinton and Barack Obama. He added, "More battles are lost by loss of hope than loss of blood."

That meant paying attention to the common man, from recognizing his soldiers' valor with medals, to giving economic progress to the middle class back home. He did his best to make his wars pay for themselves. His first levy on his enemies in Milan, Italy, in 1796, alienated the Italian population but cemented the loyalty of troops who hadn't seen cash for years. Napoleon promoted war as a profit-making enterprise and, like any Mafia don, dipped his beak to take his own share. He was rich by the end of that first Italian campaign.

His war-for-profit scheme only worked so long as victories were impressive and cheap. As conflict ground on and the toll in blood and treasure rose, the cost of war exceeded its benefits and Bonaparte's popularity sank.

The masses are practical, too.

Accordingly, Napoleon never counted on automatic acclaim. "The crowd which follows me with admiration would run with the same eagerness were I marching to the guillotine," he observed.

Pragmatism! Realizing that economic inequality and resentment of the unfairness of birth had fueled revolution, he oversaw the development of a detailed civil code, or Code Napoleon, that brought fairness to French law. Versions of it are still in use in forty countries around the world.

The Code Napoleon was exhaustive in detail because it had to deal with hundreds of practical legal problems. A constitution, in contrast, "should be short and obscure," Napoleon said, to allow flexibility to new circumstances.

He did not pretend to be inventive. Bonaparte never claimed strategic or tactical innovation, but rather the application of timeless military principle.

"The art of war is simple," he said. "Everything is a matter of execution."

Much of his campaign energy went into arithmetic. "When an enemy is superior in number," he said, "it is essential to avoid battle."

We've all seen movies of colorfully uniformed Napoleonic soldiers lined up on the battlefield, cavalry trotting and guns puffing smoke. War in those days had pomp and majesty, and the inaccuracy of firearms meant it was possible to survive a gallant charge. British and French experts calculated it took approximately four hundred bullets to inflict each enemy casualty on a confused, smoky battlefield. War was risky, but it could pay off for the officers and enlisted men who survived. Glory was a reasonable bet.

Getting to that colorful payoff was complicated and tedious, however, and so Napoleon said he wanted officers "who could count." When Confederate General Nathan Bedford Forrest said the secret to winning was "getting there firstus with the mostest," he was echoing Napoleon. Achieving that in the nineteenth century took considerable calculation.

Roads were miserable, alternately either frozen, muddy, or dusty. Increasingly huge armies had to spread far apart on country lanes to have room to march, but then had to concentrate for battle. Transportation with wagons, caissons, and carts was laborious. The vehicles had to negotiate rocks and rivers. Wheels broke. Axles snapped. The animals that pulled them had to be fed along with men, and grass wasn't always available. It was difficult to bring along enough food and water for the soldiers, let alone animals. Foraging was essential, but angered the peasants who bore the confiscations.

A commander had to allow for sickness, injury, straggling, and desertion. Weapons were so inaccurate that a battle required huge volumes of ammunition. "Each gun should have with it three hundred rounds," Napoleon wrote. "This is about the complement for two battles."

Accordingly, good officers had to be able to calculate how many men could move where, and when. To put a battery of six cannon on the battlefield with ammunition and supplies required trains totaling a hundred horses. When and where would these animals be obtained, fed, and watered? (Napoleon was cursed his entire career with too few horses.) Marching armies needed camping spots with water supplies. How to time them while coordinating the final showdown?

Count, count, count. Bonaparte's mastery was his ability to keep many variables in his head. Superiority was the product of methodical practicality that extended back days, weeks, and months. Each chess piece had to be marched exactly so far, each day, so that when the armies collided Napoleon had numerical advantage. At the same time, he constantly modified the original plan to cope with enemy maneuvers and unforeseen events.

Bonaparte's practicality extended to a cynically realistic view of human society. He developed a secret police force that paid French citizens to spy on their neighbors, and then two additional police forces so the police could spy on each other. Even then, he treated their reports with skepticism.

"The police invent more than they detect," he said.

His skepticism extended to the Catholic Church of his boyhood. "I am surrounded by priests who repeat incessantly that their kingdom is not of this world, and yet they lay hands on everything they can get," he complained.

"Religion," he allowed, "is excellent stuff for keeping common people quiet."

And, "Religion is what keeps the poor from murdering the rich."

By necessity, Napoleon knew how to work a room. But his self-aggrandizement, ego, and aggression meant he struggled to achieve true loyalty and affection. Napoleon the icon was admired by millions, but Napoleon the man was the object of wary respect and jealousy. He was hardheaded about this, too, and held subordinates in orbit for two decades by a shrewd combination of carrot and stick. He could make his generals rich or he could dismiss them, and they knew it.

But just as he could never be entirely trusted, he could never trust.

"Friends must always be treated as if one day they might be enemies," he warned.

This dire realism didn't leave much emotional satisfaction. "Happy moments are rare in the life of those who are called to the government of man," Napoleon concluded. But this too was pragmatic.

His approach has become the modern norm: Don't assume, count. Don't trust, verify. Don't rely on loyalty, rely on followers' self-interest. And for a leader, success is so yesterday. If you want to keep your crown, what have you done for your followers or customers today?

Napoleon viewed humankind through the prism of his own personality. "A celebrated people lose dignity upon a closer view. Men would have to be exceptional rascals to be as bad as I assume them to be."

And, "The herd seek out the great not for their sake but for their influence; and the great welcome them out of vanity or need."

Blunt, pithy, true.

Napoleon acknowledged how hard it is to truly know another. "It is a truth that man is difficult to know and that, if we may not deceive ourselves, we must judge him by his actions of the moment, and for that moment only."

This caution came from bitter experience. Bonaparte was devastated when told in Egypt of Josephine's immediate infidelity after their marriage. His brother Lucien helped elevate Napoleon to power, but then broke with him over principles. His brother Jerome married a Baltimore beauty against Napoleon's wishes; the emperor had the marriage annulled. Napoleon's sister Caroline thought she and her husband Joachim Murat would make a better ruling couple, and betrayed him in the end. So did other key appointees such as Fouché and Talleyrand. Plotters tried to assassinate Napoleon at least ten times. Napoleon's inability to get along with Marshal Jean-Baptiste Bernadotte meant that Bernadotte turned on him from his new position as crown prince of Sweden, allowing Russia to count on the safety of their northern flank.

Napoleon committed his own adulteries and betrayals, and his enemies regarded him a criminal megalomaniac. He saw himself forced to ruthlessness in order to win, rule, and survive. In speaking of army massacres, he commented, "Many commit a reprehensible act who are at bottom honorable men, because man seldom acts upon a natural impulse, but from some secret passion of the moment which lies hidden and concealed within the narrowest folds of his heart."

Was he speaking of himself? "Are there not spots upon the sun?" he asked.

He certainly had a wry view of his adopted country. "The French complain of everything, and always." Accordingly, he perceived limits to regulation. "We must acknowledge human weakness and bend to it, rather than combat it," he warned.

And, more pointedly, "One should never forbid what one lacks the power to prevent."

In his study of human nature, Napoleon did not confuse mercy with softness. "The act of policing is, in order to punish less often, to punish more severely."

He was not impressed with ideologues, and abhorred extremism. "There is no place in a fanatic's head where reason may enter."

Nor was he a fan of pointless sacrifice. "It is the cause, not the death, that makes the martyr."

Such relentless commonsense helps explain why Napoleon retained power for so long. He was an unusually sensible dictator. While he emphasized merit, order, and fairness, he cautioned against expecting it in others. "Sentiment rules the world, and he who fails to take that into account can never hope to lead."

But that provided opportunity. "We are here to guide public opinion, not to discuss it." The masses, Bonaparte said, "must be guided without noticing it."

How to do so? "A man will fight harder for his interests than for his rights." Napoleon assumed most people were motivated by money, security, pride, vanity, and the chance of promotion. Ideals were abstractions.

It was Benjamin Franklin who said, "Three can keep a secret if two of them are dead."

Napoleon amended, "The best way to keep one's word is not to give it."

RULE 9
ATTACK!

A fter Napoleon's defeat in Russia in 1812, his enemies – Britain, Prussia, Russia and Austria – closed in for the kill. A series of titanic and bloody battles in 1813 and 1814 eventually ended with the Allied occupation of Paris, Napoleon's abdication, restoration of the Bourbon monarchy, and Bonaparte's exile to the Mediterranean island of Elba. Of his family, all but his sister Pauline abandoned him.

Napoleon tolerated the boredom of exile for a few months, decided confinement was no life at all, and gambled one last time on the tactic that had served him so well in the past.

Attack!

He left Elba and landed in France. When troops were sent to arrest him, Napoleon opened his coat and dared them to shoot. Instead, they rallied to his side. Marshal Michel Ney promised to "put Bonaparte in a cage," but instead rejoined him. King Louis fled, Napoleon reentered Paris, reinstated his government, and the allied powers scrambled to recall their armies. Once more, audacity had worked.

Still, Napoleon's long-range strategic position looked hopeless. France was surrounded, politically divided, exhausted, and outnumbered three or four to one.

So Napoleon attacked.

Rather than wait to be squeezed by the boa constrictor of advancing enemy troops, Napoleon decided his only chance was to once more seize the initiative and defeat the enemy piecemeal.

A younger Napoleon might have pulled it off. He did manage to send the Prussians reeling, maneuvered his army between the Germans and British in Belgium, and assaulted the Duke of Wellington at Waterloo. Furious French attacks almost broke the English line. Bonaparte's subordinate generals failed to keep the Prussians at bay, however. German reinforcements finally arrived to help Wellington, Napoleon's last charge collapsed, and the French army disintegrated.

Waterloo was far from Napoleon's best day – he was ill, weary and without tactical flair – but the aggressive campaign strategy summed up his military philosophy.

"A great captain marches boldly to meet the attack," he preached. "By this means he disconcerts his adversary. We must either strike or be stricken."

To Napoleon's credit, he did not follow his attack credo blindly. His preference for the offensive was only when he had a clear chance of success. Advance prudently. Don't wait for the enemy, but don't be rash, either. Simple, eh?

The hardest thing in the world.

Napoleon said he knew little more about war at the end

of his career than the beginning. Its principles were timeless, easy to understand, but extremely difficult to apply amid difficult terrain, unpredictable weather, and the chaos of battle.

So he got to the nut of the matter. "Two armies are two bodies which meet and try to frighten each other," he explained. The force that panics first loses.

How to induce panic? Any number of things – numbers, morale, artillery, or position – could make one army more frightening than another. Napoleon used them all. He expected to profit from combat confusion.

"The battlefield is a scene of constant chaos," he said. "The winner will be the one who controls that chaos, both his own and the enemy's."

Napoleon reasoned that the aggressor could choose the point of attack and maneuver to outnumber the enemy there. If he was the defender, in contrast, the enemy could attack him where he was most vulnerable. So his campaigns are filled with examples of attacking to bring superior numbers to bear against surprised and flat-footed enemies.

"I have destroyed the enemy merely by marches," he boasted.

His subordinate General Pierre Augereau moved his corps fifty miles in thirty-six hours in Italy. General Louis-Nicolas Davout hurried ninety miles in forty-eight hours to support the French at Austerlitz.

"The nature of strategy consists of always having more forces at the point of attack, or at the point where one is being attacked by the enemy."

Early in his career he had highly trained armies that could march swiftly and quickly converge on a target. Later, as casualties mounted, training time eroded, and his armies were filled with less-motivated conscripts and foreign troops, he had to resort to battles of attrition. There he lost. He could not match enemy manpower.

Napoleon also preached that it was cheaper to go forward than backward. "However skillfully effected a retreat may be, it always lessens the morale of the army," he said. "In battle, the enemy loses practically as much as you do, while in a retreat you lose and he does not."

His tactical method was to soften up an enemy army with artillery fire, break through with a concentrated infantry attack, and then pursue with cavalry.

"Audacity succeeds as often as it fails," Napoleon reasoned. "In life it has an even chance." In his 1797 Italian campaign he was caught with a small detachment of 1,200 men surprised by three thousand Austrians. He bluffed by demanding the enemy's immediate surrender, issuing orders pretending he had more troops nearby. The ruse worked, and the superior Austrians laid down their arms to the more audacious French.

In the Austerlitz campaign, the French seized a key bridge across the Danube by lying to the Austrians that the war was over. The enemy hesitated, and the French marched across.

"If the art of war were nothing but the art of avoiding risks, glory would go to the mediocre," Napoleon said.

He nonetheless tried to consider every eventuality. "Gain time when your strength is inferior," he said. "A general should ask himself frequently, 'What would I do if the enemy's army appeared now in my front, or on my right, or on my left?' If he has any difficulty in answering these questions, his position is bad, and he should seek to remedy it."

Napoleon always tried to remain one step ahead. "It is

necessary to foresee everything the enemy may do, and to be prepared with the necessary means to counteract it." He added, "When you have resolved to fight a battle, collect your own force. A single battalion sometimes decides the day."

He didn't heed such advice before the 1800 Battle of Marengo, when he split his forces to pursue an Austrian army he wrongly believed was in retreat. Instead the Austrians attacked, and it was only the last-minute arrival of reinforcements from General Louis Desaix – who had been sent off on a wild goose chase – that saved the victory. Desaix was killed.

Napoleon learned from such mistakes and learned to wait for enemy blunders. "Never do what the enemy wishes you to do."

Bonaparte adapted. At the Battle of the Pyramids in Egypt in 1798, he used the tactical and firepower superiority of European infantry squares against out-of-date enemy Mameluke cavalry. At Ulm in 1805, he fooled the enemy by pretending to advance through the Black Forest, a feint that pinned the Austrians to their defenses while he swiftly surrounded them. At Jena and Auerstädt, he used a nineteenth century version of blitzkrieg against hesitant Prussians. One hundred sixty thousand superbly trained French soldiers defeated a quarter-million Germans by a surprise march of three parallel columns through the Franconian forest. The French inflicted two hundred thousand casualties and seized over four thousand artillery pieces, at the cost of fifteen thousand dead and wounded. On October 27, 1806, less than two months after the campaign started, Napoleon was in Berlin.

"The strength of any army is estimated by multiplying the mass by the rapidity," he said, echoing the principles of Isaac

Newton or a football lineman. "Strategy is the art of making use of time and space. Space we can recover, lost time, never."

Napoleon's early brilliance eroded. "Never attack a position in front you can gain by turning," he counseled, but then he made costly head-on charges at disasters such as Borodino and Waterloo. Just as corporations can become clumsier as they grow too big, Napoleon was less adroit when his empire swelled, his armies bloated, and he couldn't be everywhere at once. His massive empire spread his own talent too thin, and he needed good lieutenants.

RULE 10
HIRE AND INSPIRE

Napoleon relied on subordinates to protect and manage his empire and to provide a core of loyal support.

"My motto has always been: A career open to all talents, without the distinctions of birth," he said. This was the revolutionary credo that made France particularly effective in the Napoleonic era. In 1808 Bonaparte recreated a nobility to replace that mostly wiped out by the French Revolution, but it was nobility by appointment, not birth. Some 78 percent of the counts, barons and chevaliers he named came from the working and middle classes.

This meant Napoleon had to be a good judge of people, and he didn't rate competence on honeyed words. "He who knows how to flatter also knows how to slander," he warned.

"Speeches pass away, but acts remain."

Bonaparte was not infallible in his selections. Some of his

generals performed poorly, and some of his ministers were disloyal. The aloof, crafty Fouché was dismissed and reappointed as police minister four different times by an exasperated Napoleon, who needed him as much as he distrusted him.

The fact that many were promoted until they reached a level of incompetence did not surprise the emperor, however. "The most difficult art is not in the choice of men," he said, "but in giving to the men chosen the highest service of which they are capable."

Like a Mafia don, he built a loyal cadre. He created twenty-three dukes, 193 counts, and 643 barons. He distributed sixteen million francs in rewards among his 824 generals. Siblings and in-laws became kings and built fabulous fortunes. His brother Joseph became king of Spain, brother Louis king of Holland, and brother Jerome king of Westphalia, in present-day Germany. Brother-in-law Joachim Murat replaced Joseph as king of Naples.

Napoleon kept appointees at odds with each other to create tension and balance, with himself as the fulcrum. His marshals competed for his favor. His common soldiers strove for inclusion in the Imperial Guard and, for extraordinary deeds, to his newly created Legion of Honor. He invited surviving former nobility back to France after their revolutionary exile to politically balance former Jacobin revolutionaries, but refused to restore the aristocrats' wealth and property. Just as he placed his army in the middle of enemy advances, so he placed himself in the middle of France's political spectrum.

Bonaparte invited the Catholic Church back to satisfy the religious masses, but severely limited its wealth, power, and control of education.

This organizational tension didn't make Napoleonic France an easy place to be. It was a military dictatorship with a war economy and Bonaparte as micro-manager, producing thousands of letters on the most insignificant details. But it sustained internal order for fifteen years, after a previous decade of revolutionary chaos.

Hiring good people wasn't enough, Napoleon said. There had to be clarity in what they were expected to do. "An order that can be misunderstood will be misunderstood," he warned. "The secret of war lies in the communications."

A leader must be clear, concise, and consistent. "Uncertainty is painful for all people, and for all men."

As an example, "There are in Europe many good generals, but they see too many things at once. I see one thing, namely the enemy's main body. I try to crush it, confident that secondary matters will then settle themselves."

Nor was it enough to focus on high-ranking deputies and his army. Napoleon put a great deal of thought into motivating populations. "It is in the workshops of the country that the most successful war is waged against an enemy," he observed.

Bonaparte was necessarily paranoid after early assassination attempts by royalist intriguers, but he tried not to bring distrust into everyday management. One of his wonderfully judicious maxims is, "Never ascribe to malice that which can adequately be explained by incompetence."

But this comment also reveals his impatience with people not as able, and he struggled to delegate. "If you want a thing done well, do it yourself," he grumbled.

Napoleon put great effort into military reorganization. His armies had no technological edge. The design of the basic

French infantry musket was three decades old when he came to power, and went largely unchanged for his entire reign. The same was true of artillery and ship design. But he was the first in the Napoleonic Wars to effectively mass cannon firepower on the battlefield, and he created the Corps system. This allowed huge armies to be broken into subordinate units that had infantry, artillery, cavalry, and supply combined, allowing them to operate independently and making it easier for great masses of men to be maneuvered effectively. Bonaparte improved the medical corps to boost morale and paid attention to the practicalities of boots, uniforms, packs, tents, and transport.

His strengths were also his weaknesses. "Nothing is so important in war as undivided command," he said. But his distrust of war councils, his need to decide everything, and his insistence on leading from the field meant that his marshals were unprepared when left to themselves. They often underperformed. Napoleon couldn't be everywhere at once.

He did recognize the importance of paying attention to the lower ranks. "Soldiers generally win battles and generals get credit for them," Napoleon said. "The army is the true nobility of our country."

So Napoleon emphasized spirit. "An army's effectiveness depends on its size, training, experience, and morale, and morale is worth more than any of the other factors combined." He made soldiers hope and believe.

Yet for a conqueror, he was surprisingly philosophic about the long-term weakness of force and coercion. "There are in the world two powers," he said, "the sword and spirit. The spirit has always vanquished the sword."

And, "Force is the law of animals. Men are ruled by conviction."

How to convince people to follow Napoleon's lead?

Bonaparte benefitted early from revolutionary zeal. Many soldiers endorsed their cause. But inspiration became elusive as the years rolled on, deaths mounted, and his armies were increasingly populated by foreign troops from conquered countries. Each year the number of French conscripts grew as well. Between 1805 and 1813, Napoleon drafted 2.4 million unwilling soldiers.

So he thought deeply about fear, courage, and incentive. "I make my battle plans from the spirit of my sleeping soldiers," he said.

"Courage is like love," Napoleon said. "It must have hope for nourishment." His soldiers' hope was victory, the safety that follows victory, plus glory, plunder, adventure, and respect. They could become men. They would earn close comrades. They would travel and become sophisticated compared to their farm-bound neighbors. They would have tales to tell, women to impress, and memories to savor.

Nonetheless, "The French soldier is more difficult to lead than any other. He is not a machine to be put in motion but a reasonable being that must be directed."

Common soldiers could petition him. He decided their requests quickly, and explained himself if the answer was, "No." In an era when the "big hats" in almost every army were lordly and remote, this direct touch was extraordinary.

"Severe to the officers, kindly to the men," Napoleon counseled. The higher ranks had privilege, but with it went responsibility and criticism. The lower ranks had less comfort, but counted on Napoleon's rapport and support.

In exile in St. Helena, Napoleon claimed to have written a proclamation for his Army of Italy in 1796 that inspired the troops. He'd already informed the Directory in Paris of the dire state of his force: "The army is in frightening penury," he wrote. "Misery has led to indiscipline, and without discipline there can be no victory."

The resulting proclamation may be apocryphal, but it illustrates the melodrama that Napoleon knew men would respond to.

"Soldiers! You are naked, ill-fed; though the Government owe you much, it can give you nothing. Your patience, the courage you have shown amidst these rocks, are admirable; but they procure you no glory, no fame shines upon you. I want to lead you into the most fertile plains in the world. Rich provinces, great cities will be in your power; you will find their honor, glory, and riches. Soldiers of the Army of Italy, will you lack courage or steadfastness?"

Flatter. Promise. Appeal to both the soldiers' self-respect, and their greed. And then deliver.

The best soldiers who survived could look forward to promotion to the Imperial Guard with better pay, equipment, and the prospect of being held in reserve until the key moment. "It is the height of injustice not to pay a veteran more than a recruit," Bonaparte said.

Yet Napoleon was also careful to integrate his elite soldiers with new ones. He created units in which eight veterans would be joined with eight recruits so that the latter could benefit from experience.

As usual, the emperor also had his cynical side.

"Men are led by trifles," Napoleon said. "Give me enough

medals and I'll win you any war. A soldier will fight long and hard for a bit of colored ribbon."

He was not necessarily insulting the intelligence of the men he led, because Bonaparte recognized that people seek purpose. "We are all destined to die," he preached. "Can a few days of life equal the happiness of dying for one's country?" And, "If fifty thousand men were to die for the good of the state, I certainly would weep for them, but political necessity comes before everything else."

Napoleon never died for France, of course. While he re-marked much later that he should have succumbed in Russia, his instincts were to prevail. Two half-hearted suicide attempts by poison, at his two abdications in 1814 and 1815, failed without much regret on his part. Yet he did frame life as brief existence in a historical pageant in which one's deeds and accomplishments gave meaning. Flags and medals were symbols of honor, courage, and achievement. The loss of eagle-topped standards should bring deep shame to a regiment. Exemplary regimental courage, in contrast, might be summed up in a phrase sewn onto a unit flag. Captured enemy standards were proudly displayed in Paris like trophies. A wound was a badge of honor.

"Orders and decorations are necessary in order to dazzle the people."

He seemed to carry no guilt for the havoc his ambition caused, and no hesitation in demanding sacrifices. "The first qualification of a soldier is fortitude under fatigue and priva-tion," he said. "Courage is only the second; hardship, poverty, and want are the best school for the soldier."

Or, to put it another way, "Courage isn't having the strength to go on – it is going on when you don't have the strength."

Bonaparte was also not the type to hug or wail. "A man like me troubles himself little about a million men," he declared. (Although frequently quoted as evidence of Napoleon's indifference to human life, he made this statement to Austrian minister Klemens von Metternich in 1813 as bluster, to warn of his determination should Austria go to war against him. The Austrians did anyway.)

Napoleon once told an odd but revealing story of coming upon a dead soldier being nuzzled by his pet dog. "Tearless, I had given orders which brought death to thousands," he recalled. "Yet here I was stirred, profoundly stirred, stirred to tears. And by what? By the grief of one dog."

Putting Napoleon on the psychiatrist's couch gives us a patient of emotional repression, a man with a weird distancing from the consequences of his relentless ambition. Being moved by a dog and not by human slaughter suggests one very remote, very buttoned-up dude. The sorrow that furrowed the face of Abraham Lincoln never showed up on Napoleon's features.

But he also inspired in a way few leaders have ever matched. Which brings us to one of his most controversial rules.

RULE 11
NECESSARY RUTHLESSNESS?

"**B**loodletting is among the ingredients of political medicine," Napoleon said. Not a surprising sentiment from the man who mowed down a Paris mob with a "whiff of grapeshot." His medical analogy is a reference to the practice of bleeding patients to cure them, which still existed in Bonaparte's time.

His point was that violence is a means to a political end, and brutal violence may reach that end more quickly. This is always the justification of dictators, which makes Napoleon debatable in the extreme. There is a difference between sternness and brutality, and Bonaparte arguably crossed it at times.

Most leaders are required to do difficult things, from ordering men into battle to, in the corporate world, firing, laying off, or favoring one person over another with promotion. Napoleon roamed the spectrum between being firm to being mean, and from calculation to callousness.

"He who cannot look over a battlefield with a dry eye causes the death of many men uselessly," he argued. To Bonaparte, fear, doubt, pity, and hesitation were the enemies of victory, and the lack of decisive victory needlessly prolonged war. Ruthlessness *saved* lives, instead of squandering them.

"If you wage war," he said, "do it energetically and with severity. This is the only way to make it shorter and consequently less inhuman."

Similarly, shortly after he seized power he ordered harshness toward the rebellious province of Vendée as necessary surgery to cure internal restiveness. (This was the same place he had declined to subdue himself, as a young general.)

"The First Consul (Napoleon) believes that it would serve as a salutary example to burn down two or three large communes chosen among those whose conduct is worst," he wrote to his commanders, referring to himself in the third person. "Experience has taught him that a spectacularly severe act is, in the conditions you are facing, the most humane method. Only weakness is inhumane."

The villages were burned, rebels arrested or shot, and within a month the province had quieted. Did his calculus save more lives than it cost?

Bonaparte used the same ruthlessness against revolts in Italy and Cairo.

When Italian peasants rose against his occupation, he shot one hundred of them and burned the village of Binasco. He also leveled the house of a priest who had rallied the rebels, and melted down the church bells that had summoned the peasants to revolt. End of uprising.

He confessed some guilt, but added to his officers, "Nothing is more salutary than appropriately severe examples."

When Egyptians rose against the French occupation of Cairo, his army responded by killing 2,500 rebels and piling their heads in Ezbekyeh Square. "Every night we cut off thirty heads," he reported to the French government. Cairo quieted.

At Jaffa in present-day Israel, Napoleon's demand for surrender was answered by the display of his envoy's head on a pike. Napoleon responded by storming the town and allowing a frenzied French slaughter of men, women, and children that went on all night. Later, faced with Turkish prisoners he had no way to take care of, and mindful that some of them had been earlier captured and released with the promise not to fight further, Bonaparte ordered the massacre of three thousand on the edge of the Mediterranean. Criticism for the deed dogged him for the rest of his life.

Napoleon did not hesitate to shoot deserters or soldiers who committed crimes. His armies appeared to appreciate his firmness, not resent it.

From a civilian perspective, violence is abhorrent. But it probably did end some battles and revolts more quickly. At the same time, the emperor's instinct toward repression created endless enemies and repeated war. Once Bonaparte left the historical scene the world seemed to get along just fine without his draconian tactics. Europe would not see such a scale of violence for another century, when World War I broke out.

Napoleon was never as ghastly as Hitler, Stalin, or Mao. He didn't conduct genocide. He generally ruled within the law. Still, he had the brutal instincts of a hardened general who had come of age in the Reign of Terror. "Remember, gentlemen," he told his officers before the bloody battle of Smolensk, "what a Roman emperor said: 'The corpse of an enemy always smells sweet.'"

He never lost sight of the fact that he had been made by war, and never seemed particularly grateful or disturbed by the deaths of more than a million Frenchmen during his reign. Royalist conspirators were imprisoned and tortured. Political opponents were exiled as far away as South America.

"A king is sometimes obliged to commit crimes," he justified, "but they are the crimes of his position."

One such alleged crime was the March 1804 French kidnapping of Louis de Bourbon-Condé, duc d'Enghien, who was snatched from his rented home in German territory across the French border. Napoleon's police had uncovered royalist conspiracies to overthrow Bonaparte, and the duke was caught up in the hysteria. A secret midnight preemptory trial led to d'Enghien's swift execution, resulting in outrage across Europe. (Napoleon's defenders blamed the killing on his foreign minister Talleyrand.)

The execution "was worse than a crime, it was a blunder," is an assessment usually attributed to Napoleon's secret police chief, Fouché. And indeed, the incident badly damaged Bonaparte's image. He defended it by saying it was part of a necessary campaign to crush repeated royalist plots against him, including the explosion of a barrel of gunpowder in a Paris street that had narrowly missed Napoleon and Josephine on Christmas Eve, 1800.

In yet another example of violent cruelty, Napoleon's generals ruthlessly (and unsuccessfully) tried to suppress the Haitian slave revolt with drownings, hunting dogs, and torture. The slave general Touissant L'Ouverture was tricked into capture and imprisoned in the French Alps where he died in a dank cell. The draconian measures ultimately failed, however, and the black revolt triumphed.

And of course Bonaparte prosecuted bloody and pitiless wars in Spain beginning in 1808 and Russia in 1812. The more his army tried to repress the population, the more guerillas rose to oppose them. The painter Goya immortalized the horror of French reprisals against Spanish rebels.

Why so ruthless? Early in his career, Napoleon witnessed mob massacres of royalist guards in Paris and of royalist defenders in Toulon. After his victory in Toulon, hundreds were shot or guillotined on order of Napoleon's revolutionary masters. His conclusion? "It is better to eat than be eaten."

"In my youth I had illusions," he said. "I got rid of them fast."

Napoleon argued he was judicious. "Cruelty can only be justified by necessity," he said.

But there is no question that he viewed himself above ordinary custom, and blundered because of it.

"Morality has nothing to do with such a man as I am," he once contended. He said this to justify his infidelities to Josephine, but he would have applied this self-absolution to massacres as well.

A reader can get a sense of his realism – or cynicism – from a sampling of his statements:

- "Men are moved by two levers only: fear and interest."

- "Men are more easily governed through their vices than their virtues."

- "If you wish to be a success in the world, promise everything, deliver nothing."

- "You don't reason with intellectuals, you shoot them."

Napoleon's occasional mercies and hesitations sometimes belie his own words, making one wonder if his grim quips were intended to shock and entertain as much as instruct. But he prided himself on his lack of sentimentality. "The heart of a statesman must be in his head."

As a result, he sometimes sounds like a modern political consultant. "In politics, never retreat, never retract, never admit a mistake," he advised.

Such "realism" colored his view of the world. "The surest way to remain poor is to be honest," he declared.

He remarked that he had few true friends, and he always distrusted. "The allies we gain by victory will turn against us upon the bare whisper of our defeat," he warned. After the Russian disaster, this turned out to be true.

And, "Better to have a known enemy than a forced ally."

Napoleon's ruthless instincts were in part the result of frustration from fighting the same alliances again and again. He beat five coalitions over a bloody decade, before being defeated by the last two.

"When you have an enemy in your power," he said, "deprive him of the means of ever injuring you." In that, he failed. He repeatedly defeated Austria. He punished it by demanding indemnities. He restricted the size of its army. He married into its royal family. But the defiant nation warred with him again and again.

Keeping people conquered is an exhausting and endless task. Empires don't last, and Napoleon's was shorter than most. Here, he brought his realism to bear once again.

"Alexander, Caesar, Charlemagne, and I have founded empires," he supposedly observed, although the validity of this quote has been questioned. "But on what did we rest the creations of our genius? Upon force. Jesus Christ founded his empire upon love, and at this hour millions of men would die for him."

At least Bonaparte was not just ruthless with others. He could be ruthless in his assessment of himself.

DOMINATE AT YOUR OWN RISK

O ne of Napoleon's least attractive traits was his need to dominate others, be it nations, generals, soldiers, ministers, servants, wives, lovers, or relatives.

"The terror he inspires is inconceivable," critic Madame de Staël wrote to her father after meeting Napoleon at his brother Joseph's estate. "One has the impression of an impetuous wind blowing about one's ears when one is near that man."

The code name of Bourbon royalists for Napoleon was, "The Torrent."

He wasn't just a born leader. He was incapable of following, deferring, or partnering. And like all strong-willed people, Napoleon could be a butthead.

"Once an idea which he considered expedient lodged itself in his head," Napoleonic aide Armand Caulaincourt wrote in his memoirs, "the emperor became his own dupe. When he sought to seduce you, he had already seduced himself."

This trait, part talent and part flaw, led him to rule much of Europe. But it thwarted any realistic hope of normal satisfaction, and accumulated enemies the way the underside of a couch accumulates lint. Bonaparte's success became his failure, and his biography is a cautionary tale. If you need to *always* win then perhaps you need a psychiatrist, not an army.

One thinks of Hitler, to whom Napoleon is sometimes compared. There is a profound difference, however, between the two conquerors. Hitler hated. Napoleon did not. People were obstacles or instruments to Napoleon, but he operated from expediency, rather than sympathy or hatred. "A true man never hates," he said. "He rages, and his bad moods never last beyond the present moment." Hitler, in contrast, could not get beyond his own twisted ideology, and thus became irrational in a way Napoleon would have considered stupid. The German dictator's crimes were vastly worse, too.

Still, Bonaparte recognized his desire to dominate. "Great ambition is the passion of great character," Napoleon said. "He who is endowed with it may perform either very great actions or very bad ones; all depends upon the principles which direct him."

Napoleon's instinct for reform eventually became tangled with his personal pursuit of historical glory, and his psychological need to dominate. Yet there was method to his mania. "Public opinion is ever on the side of the strongest," he said.

And just as he didn't wait for permission from his superiors, neither did he depend on it from his followers. "In a great nation, the majority are incapable of judging wisely of things."

Who did have such wisdom? Napoleon Bonaparte.

He first needed to dominate his family. When Napoleon's father died it was he, rather than his older brother Joseph, who assumed responsibility for his mother and siblings. His brothers and sisters later helped by ruling conquered kingdoms and marrying strategically, but Napoleon was always the fount of their influence, prestige, and wealth. There was no real partnership, only domination.

The same was true of his marshals, subordinate generals, and government ministers. Bonaparte might give great responsibility and great reward to his lieutenants, but he never deferred to them or fully trusted their independence. They were his chess pieces.

Napoleon protested that his wars were only defensive, but the truth was that he was emotionally unable to tolerate a balance of power. When he had other monarchs as allies his approach was to lecture them, rather than seek advice and partnership. He was too proud, and too strong, to make the concessions necessary to sustain the 1802 temporary peace with Britain. The English were equally at fault for the breakdown of the Treaty of Amiens, but Bonaparte's instinct was for war that would let him dominate, not uneasy co-existence.

He used a variety of techniques to maintain superiority. The most important was his own competence: people deferred to Napoleon because he seemed to be able to accomplish what they could not. Another was self-assurance. Most of us aren't certain where we want to go. Bonaparte was happy to point the way, and confident of his own genius.

"Take time to deliberate," he counseled, "but when the time for action comes, stop thinking and go in."

He was the ultimate man of action. "Firmness, and above all speed, are indispensable in matters of policy."

As part of his rise, Napoleon also learned how to win respect from older, more experienced men. "A great reserve and severity of manners are necessary for the command of those who are older than ourselves," he taught.

He was known for volcanic rages that turned on and off like a tap. How much of this was uncontrolled mental tumult and how much was calculated theatrics is unclear, but again, Napoleon always had a theatrical sense of himself.

The emperor also relied on ceremony. His thrones were elevated. His troops passed in review. Cannon salutes announced victories and births. He dominated battlefields from perches on hills. His favorite horse was a distinctive white.

None of this would have worked were he incompetent. Napoleon dominated because he won. And he seemed unusually immune to self-doubt or hesitation. "The torment of precautions often exceeds the dangers to be avoided," he said. "It is sometimes better to abandon one's self to destiny."

This abandonment allowed Bonaparte to make risky decisions that would have paralyzed lesser men. Again, he trusted luck. "Fortune is like a woman. If you miss her today, think not to find her tomorrow."

And, "I saw the crown of France laying on the ground, so I picked it up with my sword."

Unfortunately, domination meant he could not easily delegate, and so Napoleon exhausted himself with micromanaging. Followers found that they could rise with Bonaparte, but his manner discouraged true loyalty. His siblings were more resentful than grateful, and fellow monarchs didn't trust him. And because he was so powerful, he didn't know when to stop.

RULE 13
DON'T OVERREACH

A hapless character in the satiric movie *This Is Spinal Tap* notes that, "It's a fine line between stupid . . . and clever."

Napoleon beat the rock star to it. "From the sublime to the ridiculous is but a step," he said when contemplating his defeat in Russia. And later, after reinforcements couldn't save one of his generals in the Dresden campaign, "From triumph to failure is only one step."

Success turned to failure because Napoleon stuck with strategies that had become obsolete. If something is working, human instinct is to do more of it – but you can have too much of a good thing. Sugar. Salt. Alcohol. Invasion. And if there is one thing we remember about Napoleon's career, it was his mistake in invading Russia. A vast army of more than six hundred thousand men was annihilated.

Until the 1812 invasion, Napoleon's enemies had

conveniently offered up their armies for destruction, after which he occupied their capitals and dictated terms. Why not try this one more time, using an invincibly huge army against the last formidable continental opponent remaining?

But for every action there is a reaction, and Bonaparte's success came back to haunt him. "You must not fight too often with one enemy," Napoleon warned, "or you will teach him your art of war."

Russia learned. Between its defeat at the battle of Friedland in 1807 and Napoleon's invasion in 1812, Russia reorganized its military on the French model, including adoption of the corps system. Prussia and Austria did the same. Of the 183 aging Prussian generals whom Napoleon faced when he easily defeated that nation in 1806, only eight remained when Prussia went back to war in 1813. Their replacements were younger, smarter, and more determined.

Moreover, the stinging defeats the allies had in the past meant they wouldn't risk the decisive battle Napoleon sought. Why not simply deny him victory by retreating into the endless territory of Russia? So when Napoleon invaded their Motherland, the Russians refused to punch it out with the champ on the border. They ran around the ring and played rope-a-dope, while Napoleon chased and fumed.

Bonaparte also reasoned that if a big army brought him past success, a gigantic army would almost guarantee victory.

Yet it was the very size of the Grand Armée that was the cause of its doom. A smaller army might have tempted the Russians to risk a battle. Napoleon's gigantic juggernaut helped persuade them to avoid one.

While the Czar's generals did make a reluctant stand at

the bloody battles of Smolensk and Borodino, they never permitted complete destruction. (Indicative of the kind of total war Napoleon had unleashed upon the world, Borodino left seventy-five thousand French and Russian casualties from a single day's fighting, including forty-three dead and wounded French generals. The two sides fired three cannonballs and seventy-seven musket balls per *second*. Nonetheless, the battle was inconclusive for both sides.)

Seizing Moscow did no good when the Russians simply burned it. The French occupied only a narrow ribbon of Russian territory that they'd stripped of food. Napoleon tried to retreat by another route so his men could forage to eat, but battle forced the French back the way they'd come. That meant they filed past the hideously decaying bodies of Borodino and the villages they had foolishly burned.

Napoleon later blamed nature, being too proud to give credit to his Russian opponents and their British allies, who throughout the Napoleonic Wars gave 66 million pounds to finance coalitions against him.

"The obstacles before which I failed did not proceed from men but from the elements," he argued from exile. "In the south it was the sea that destroyed me (in naval battles such as the Nile and Trafalgar) and in the north it was the fire of Moscow and the ice of winter. So there it is, water, air, fire, all nature and nothing but nature; the problems of nature are insoluble."

No, *mon Empereur.* You went too far. You didn't know when to quit.

Technology and logistics had not advanced enough to support the Grand Army's bloated size, which was assembled right after a European crop failure in the winter of 1811-1812. His army marched into Russia with less than four weeks rations, expecting a short campaign. Long before winter approached, they were starving.

The huge assembly of six hundred thousand men from across Europe (only half were French) and a quarter-million horses created a breeding ground for disease. An estimated 140,000 soldiers died of sickness, with six thousand succumbing to typhus each *day* at the height of the plague. All the horses were lost to starvation and cold.

Napoleon didn't hug the Baltic coastline to strike the Russian capital of St. Petersburg, which might have allowed sea supply and ready retreat. Instead he followed the Russian army into the vast Russian heartland.

Such a goal wasn't really planned, another indication that Bonaparte's early brilliance was eroding. It wasn't until July 26, more than a month after the invasion began, that Napoleon finally decided to go to Moscow since he couldn't come to grips with the Russians any other way.

He ignored generals and ministers advising against the entire adventure, and didn't listen to their pleas for prudent retreat in subsequent councils of war. He wouldn't halt at Smolensk to consolidate his gains but instead hurried on, hoping for a knockout punch.

He later gave lip service to halting and wintering over. "1813 will see us in Moscow, and 1814 in St. Petersburg," he said. But he was too impatient to wait.

The French were overconfident. They weighed themselves down with looted goods. They alienated the population. Czar Alexander and the Orthodox Church were successful in painting Napoleon as an antichrist, come to ravage Mother Russia. Above all, the French expected the Russians to play their game.

When Russia refused to do so, Bonaparte had no Plan B. He went from a strategy of attack to hoping events would turn his way: the very wishing that he warned against early in his career. He ignored his own maxims, and at Borodino – where he was sick and indecisive – he wouldn't release his vaunted Guard reserve to destroy the retreating Russians at the end of the battle. He didn't know how much strength the Russians had left, and was thus reluctant to commit his last troops. As a result the occupation of Moscow was militarily meaningless, especially after the Russians set their own city on fire.

Napoleon lost a third of his army to combat casualties, and two-thirds to disease, cold, hunger, and desertion. He left behind 1,131 cannon.

Russia suffered almost as badly, losing 150,000 military dead and 300,000 wounded to the French invasion, plus huge civilian casualties. But with 46 million inhabitants, its manpower reserves were immense. Napoleon's empire had more people at its height – 82 million Europeans – but two-thirds were subjects of questionable loyalty. Many turned on France after the Russian defeat.

The same inability to come to grips with the enemy plagued him in the bloody campaigns in Germany the following year. He faced three opposing armies from Prussia, Russia, and Austria, and couldn't pin down any of them. "The man was annihilated by the presence of space," said French general Paul Thiébault.

In an earlier chapter, I quoted Napoleon's maxim that the

audacious have at least an even chance of succeeding. But he also warned, "With audacity one can undertake anything, but not *do* everything."

Successful formulas have an expiration date. The key to Napoleon's destruction had already been discovered by the Spanish, who rose up en masse beginning in 1808 to wage merciless guerilla war. There Napoleon's pride got the better of him, because he insisted on extending his Continental blockade of British trade to the Iberian Peninsula. To do so he unwisely put his brother on the Spanish throne, invaded Portugal, invited British intervention, and embroiled his army in a nineteenth century quagmire. Again, his enemies refused the decisive battle he sought and again, Napoleon wouldn't give up. The world took note.

The Peninsular War started so splendidly. Spain, which had been a reluctant ally, had become chaotic under the hapless Charles IV. French troops were welcomed to sustain order. But then the French began occupying Spanish fortresses. Charles IV abdicated in favor of his more popular son Ferdinand VII. In May, 1808, the Spanish rose spontaneously against the occupiers, the French brutally retaliated, and by August the British had landed in Portugal. Campaign followed campaign, year after year, back and forth, with losses mounting. By 1814, the British and their Spanish allies had pushed the French out of Spain and invaded southern France.

"It was the Spanish War that overthrew me," Napoleon said. "All my disasters can be traced back to this fatal knot."

Don't overreach. It is instructive to examine historical maps of France's boundaries at the start and end of Napoleon's career. The borders after Waterloo were back where they had been twenty-three years before. All those dead – and for what?

Invasion fit Napoleon's pugnacious personality. If ambition was part of his essential being, as he said, so was aggression. Such a trait was an advantage on the battlefield, but a handicap in sustaining an empire. He could not bring himself to trade conquered territories for peace, and so war followed war. He couldn't compromise, bargain, or moderate.

With his philosophy to strike instead of being struck, he created a vicious cycle. Each victory created new enemies and resentments, and the only way to avoid revenge and retaliation was to strike again, and again, and again. The more Napoleon pummeled the Austrians, Prussians, and Russians, the more determined they were to seek his overthrow. The more he defeated them, the more they learned and the harder they fought.

Had Napoleon demonstrated more patience, and been willing to consolidate his empire by making concessions to buy peace, he might have achieved a permanently dominant France. But he sounded petulant and juvenile.

"You do not get peace by shouting peace," he complained. "Peace is a meaningless word; what we need is a glorious peace."

By which he meant a peace that favored France and Napoleon. He had a chance to keep Austria out of the Sixth Coalition that defeated him in 1813 and 1814 by giving back their Adriatic provinces. He couldn't bring himself to do it. Later, he had a chance for peace by giving up Belgium, Holland, and Italy. He couldn't accept that, either. So the allies advanced to Paris and he was forced to abdicate.

In the 1813 campaigns, he wasted time and men trying to retake Berlin when the city had no strategic value. The only purpose was to humiliate Prussia. The younger Napoleon cared only for destroying the enemy army, and lectured his brother-in-law Murat on the empty glory of seizing Vienna. The older Napoleon had too much pride.

Later, when he was so desperate that he was ready to agree to anything, it was much too late.

His constant war making had created a monster. At the three-day Battle of Leipzig in 1813, 203,000 French faced 362,000 allied soldiers, a titanic collision that left 85,000 French casualties. War had gone from being profitable, which it was in 1796 Italy, to being insane.

Napoleon had the instincts of a bully, but sensed his own essential flaw. In 1805, near the height of his success, he commented, "A man has his day in war as in other things; I myself shall be good for it another six years, after which even I shall have to stop."

Seven years later, he invaded Russia.

RULE 14
NEVER STOP LEARNING

N apoleon studied and learned all his life. Upon being appointed to command the Army of Italy in 1796, he read everything he could about the theater in which he would campaign. He peppered officers who had served there with queries, unafraid to reveal his ignorance by asking dumb questions. As a result, he arrived on campaign with the astuteness necessary to handle the complex politics of the Italian peninsula. He similarly crammed for his invasion of Egypt, reading all he could find on the Muslim world. Knowledge, he believed, gave him an edge.

Napoleon admired scholars. He got himself elected to the Institute de France as a mathematician in 1797 so he could converse with the leading scientists of the day. When he invaded Egypt in 1798, he brought 167 scientists, engineers, and artists with his army, founding the discipline of Egyptology.

He was determined that all of France would share his thirst for information. "The most honorable as well as the most useful occupation of all nations is to contribute to the extension of human knowledge," he said.

In an 1807 meeting on the French education system, he stated, "Of all our institutions, public education is the most important. Everything depends on it, the present and the future. It is essential that the morals and political ideas of the generation now growing up should no longer be dependent upon the news of the day or the circumstances of the moment. Above all we must secure unity: we must be able to cast a whole generation in the same mold."

Napoleon centralized control of education under an Imperial University. There were Catholic elementary schools for basic education, state secondary schools that directed students toward either government service or the military, and boarding schools with an intense six-year program for the most promising intellectuals.

"Public instruction should be the first object of government," he said.

Because up to a third of the French population was deficient in French at the time of the Revolution, Napoleon required officers and non-commissioned officers to speak the tongue. It was common for foreign officers to sign on in their search for employment and advancement, and so this order was essential for army communication.

He also encouraged, or at least tolerated, debate and discussion. "I am never angry when contradicted; I seek to be enlightened," he contended. One suspects not all his generals and aides would agree – he was famous for the occasional rage and stubbornness – but he did encourage subordinates to speak up, while always reserving the final decision to himself.

He read voraciously as a young man, tried his hand at writing adventure stories and romances, and prized literate conversations. He was thrilled to spend a day with the German author Goethe. His favorite work when young was a cycle of Scottish poems by a bard named Ossian. The work was a medieval fantasy epic with dramatic deaths and mistaken identities. Other favorites included Plutarch's *The Lives of Noble Grecians and Romans,* Machiavelli, Voltaire, Montesquieu, Moliere, Rousseau, Racine, Buffon's *Natural History,* and Goethe's tale of suicide, *The Sorrows of Young Werther,* which Napoleon read several times. A choice when he arrived in Paris for military school was *Gil Blas,* about a penniless Spanish boy who rises to the top. Bonaparte's own youthful writing was melodramatic, its purple prose teeming with heroes, tragedy, sacrifice, and thwarted love.

"A diversity of reading pleases the imagination as much as the diversity of sounds pleases the ear," he said. "Show me a family of readers, and I will show you the people who move the world."

As much as he desired military empire, he appears to have recognized how difficult it is to sustain. "In the long run, the sword is always beaten by the mind."

But not necessarily quickly. "Truth will always prevail in the long run, but how slow its progress!"

Napoleon himself was sometimes slow to promote technological gain. His military weapons remained stuck in the eighteenth century. His government rejected American Robert Fulton's early designs for a steamboat and submarine, driving the inventor to Britain. Agricultural France lagged behind industrial Britain in adoption of the steam engine and the launch of the industrial revolution.

Napoleon's censorship did little to promote literature or journalism during his reign.

Still, "The only victories which leave no regret are those which are gained over ignorance," he said.

RULE 15
REMEMBER THE HOME FRONT

S ome historians contend Napoleon was two hundred years ahead of his time in his dream of a united Europe with a common currency, laws, and trade. Others argue he was a hundred years behind, confusing unity with empire.

The difference between Napoleon's empire and today's European Union is that Bonaparte's creation was a conglomeration of states under his dictatorial control, organized to benefit France. Subject countries, which included much of present-day Belgium, the Netherlands, Switzerland, Germany, Croatia, and Italy, had to supply soldiers and money. Everyone was subject to his will.

But Napoleon believed he could bring new freedoms and promote commerce by imposing reforms, improving transportation, and lowering trade barriers. Unfortunately, economic understanding was primitive in Napoleon's day and his protectionist policies didn't work well.

His own economic theory started with equality and merit under his authoritarian control. "Democracy, if it is reasonable, limits itself to give everyone an equal opportunity to compete and obtain," he said.

In Napoleon's view, human beings desire two incompatible goals: equality, and distinction. We all want to be equal, but many of us secretly want to be "more equal" than others, to be above average, to win.

The masses desire equality, he said, but, "They would gladly renounce it if everyone could entertain the hope of rising to the top. What must be done, then, is to give everybody the hope of being able to rise."

Bonaparte himself seemed the preeminent example. Here was a Corsican outsider who ruled an empire. His story was as dazzling as that of today's billionaires and superstars. But he contradicted his own philosophy and biography by replacing the revolutionary "citizen" of merit with a new nobility, dominated by his own family, that would deny any other upstart soldier from following him to power. Rather than devising a competitive system to identify the most able successor, the emperor fell back on the old European dynastic model. His infant son would inherit. The youthful revolutionary had turned, after success, into a conservative reactionary.

Nonetheless, Napoleon did do a better job of economic opportunity than previous royals. When he seized power in 1799, France's economy was a wreck after royalist debt and ten years of revolution and turmoil. Its credit was ruined. Business was moribund, hampered by political and military uncertainty. Paris had declined in population.

Bonaparte swiftly brought order and national security,

repaired economic confidence, and attracted people back to the capital. He did so, however, with a dictatorial hand that prohibited labor unions, limited the movement of workers by requiring passbooks to travel, and outlawed trade with England. He was a fiscal conservative by both instinct and necessity.

While Britain had the solvency to solicit wartime loans and keep taxes within reason, French credit was so poor that Napoleon's government was forced to balance the budget and pay its own way. He backed the new franc with gold and silver. He pushed French taxes higher than they had been before the Revolution. He imposed heavy levies on lands that he conquered. The drawback was eventual unpopularity. The ordinary Englishman fought the war on credit. The ordinary Frenchman could not.

The basic French problem was that Napoleon's military consumed half the government budget. He was determined that "war must pay for war," but this proved to be a receding rainbow. Austria was forced to contribute at least 239 million francs after multiple defeats. Prussia paid as much as 514 million francs, and Italy provided 30 million francs a year. Biographer Andrew Roberts has calculated that in total, Napoleon extracted 1.8 billion francs from conquered enemies.

But he spent 3 billion francs on his military during his reign, meaning that on balance, conquest lost money.

Some reforms worked. One of Napoleon's first successes was the creation of the Bank of France in 1800, replacing the worthless paper *assignants* created by the revolutionary governments with new paper francs backed by gold and silver. His military victories and continental plunder initially helped stabilize the economy with an influx of looted wealth.

A credit crisis in 1805 was averted by Bonaparte's victory at Austerlitz. But as his empire expanded and armies swelled, profit disappeared.

Bonaparte also authorized the construction of roads, canals, and bridges. "The indestructible pages of great reigns are the battles and the gigantic works," he said. Although the *Arc de Triomphe* in Paris was not completed until after Napoleon's death, he authorized it in 1806 at the height of his career. He opened up the Champs-Elysées by demolishing old mansion houses between the Tuileries and the Louvre, making the avenue the widest and most magnificent in Europe. He ordered other roads such as the Rue de Rivoli expanded, anticipating the wholesale nineteenth century makeover of Paris that would be designed by Baron Haussmann under Napoleon III.

The first Napoleon graced his capital with five new bridges, five new slaughterhouses, eight covered markets, fifty-six ornamental fountains to improve public water supplies, and the Canal de l'Ourcq to feed the fountains. Outside Paris, he initiated construction of twenty thousand miles of imperial roads, a thousand miles of canals, new routes across the Alps, and the dredging and improvement of several harbors.

Bonaparte controlled the price of flour and bread to prevent food riots. The export of grain was prohibited. He promoted the sugar beet industry to replace sugarcane cut off by British blockade. A food preservation competition led Nicolas Appert to invent canning. Agriculture was improved and an Industrial Board was organized.

Napoleon's new Civil Code replaced forty-two earlier property and trade codes with one, giving individuals and business legal stability. This was followed by the Code of Civil Procedure, the Code of Commercial Law, the Penal Code, and the Code of Criminal Procedure.

Less successful was Napoleon's Continental System, also known as the Berlin Decrees, his 1806 response to Britain's naval blockade of his empire.

Napoleon spent his entire rule trying to figure out a way to defeat Great Britain. Egypt was supposed to be a path to English possessions in India, but France was unable to retain its foothold there. Bonaparte's hope of invading England in 1805 was smashed for the final time by England's defeat of the French-Spanish fleet at Trafalgar. British control of the sea proved a trump card in the 23-year-long struggle between the two nations, and yet Napoleon never gave up. "Rome defeated Carthage," he insisted, meaning a land power had defeated a naval one in ancient times. He hoped conquest of Russia might eventually open an overland route to invade Britain's Asian colonies. But that failed, too.

So he came up with the idea of blocking England from European commerce. ("A nation of shopkeepers," he called his arch-rival in a letter to the Shah of Persia, borrowing a phrase originally coined by the economist Adam Smith.) The idea was to ruin its trade-based economy and choke off the subsidies Britain gave Napoleon's enemies. Each nation that came under Bonaparte's possession or influence was prohibited from trading with the island kingdom.

England *was* hurt: its exports fell by a third or more. But smugglers circumvented many of the restrictions, French allies resented the restriction, and the Continental System forced the British to expand their overseas empire in compensation.

The Napoleonic Wars ultimately made the British Empire and trade system stronger, not weaker.

France suffered as much or more from Napoleon's scheme. Food prices rose. Shipbuilding and rope making declined. Portugal's refusal to join the system led to French invasion and British rescue, which in turn helped spark the disastrous Peninsular War. Russia's resumption of British trade led to Napoleon's invasion of that country. French ports declined. Belgium and Switzerland profited more than France from the lack of British competition.

The real tragedy was that in order to continue his trade war with Britain, Napoleon could never make a lasting peace on land. Enforcing the Continental System led to war with Portugal, Spain, Russia, Prussia, and Austria, and thus seeded Bonaparte's downfall. His obsession with England resulted in a loss of strategic perspective. The man who prided himself on clear goals lost his grasp on risk and reward.

The Napoleonic Wars also distracted French energy just as the industrial revolution was getting underway. By 1815, at the end of Napoleon's reign, French industrialization was only to the level Britain had achieved in 1780.

The imperfect economic policy suggests this extraordinary man spread himself too thin. Napoleon's expertise was the battlefield and bureaucracy. In gripping the reins of power, he had limited energy and talent to promote business. Nor did he find ministers to drive the economy for him. Not much in the way of economic quotation comes down to us from Napoleon. He was a man of armies, thrones, plebiscites, and public works, but not of markets and gross domestic product.

And when the cost of endless war exceeded its benefits, his support began to evaporate.

CONCLUSION
WAS HE HAPPY?

Thomas Jefferson's memorable phrase in the American Declaration of Independence, "life, liberty, and the pursuit of happiness," never resonated with Napoleon.

His goal was to be great, not happy.

A psychiatrist might argue that glory was a roundabout way for Bonaparte to achieve satisfaction, triumph, and thus a kind of narrow happiness. Stoking ambition was what made Napoleon tick.

By such measure, maybe he was happier than most.

But he never claimed to be.

Which gets us to the point of Napoleon's life, and the point of our own. Is a successful life one of contentment, contribution, and satisfaction? Or is it measured by battles won, statues erected, money accumulated, destiny achieved, and the swankiest tomb? What should existence be about?

A life coach might judge that the French ruler's life was one gigantic miscalculation. Only power could satisfy Napoleon, but power came with the price of personal isolation, crushing responsibility, unending work, inevitable disappointment, and defeat. He endured illness, injury, divorce, and betrayal. He lost all he gained. The French borders of 1815 were no different from those at the Revolution in 1791.

Bonaparte would not necessarily disagree. "All my life I have sacrificed everything – comfort, self-interest, happiness – to my destiny," he wrote Josephine.

Would Bonaparte have been happier as a quiet bourgeois merchant, raising a family and minding his own business? Or would he have been tormented by the frustration of ambition unsatisfied?

He might have said happiness is beside the point.

"Existence is a curse, rather than a blessing," he said. "To live is to suffer."

Ouch.

His goal was to Be Somebody, still talked about in books like this one. "Ambition and the enjoyment of high offices do not constitute the happiness and satisfaction of a great man," he said. "He seeks the good opinion of the world and the esteem of posterity."

No matter if it makes millions of others miserable. To Napoleon, life was about *him*. It was battle. It was struggle. It was achievement. To win was to live.

In today's comfortably hedonistic Western society, the idea of living for posterity and reputation might strike many as odd. Even Bonaparte observed that fame is fleeting. But Napoleon, devourer of biographies of the great captains of history, chose glory as the goal of life. Tears came to his eyes when one flatterer compared him to Julius Caesar and Alexander the Great.

"Death is nothing," he said, "but to die defeated and inglorious is to die daily." He added, "Life is strewn with so many obstacles, and may be the source of so many evils, that death is not the greatest of all."

Napoleon wanted renown. "A great reputation is like a great noise, the louder it is proclaimed the further it is heard. The laws, constitutions, monuments, actions – all have their limits, but glory spreads itself through many generations."

No wonder he called his greatest victory at Austerlitz – a battle that killed and wounded tens of thousands – one of the happiest days of his life.

On St. Helena, Bonaparte reflected. "Yes, I was happy when I became First Consul, happy at the time of my marriage, and happy at the birth of the King of Rome (his son, Napoleon II.) But then I did not feel perfectly confident of the security of my position. Perhaps I was happiest at Tilsit." This was a treaty conference where he negotiated a favorable peace with Tsar Alexander of Russia in 1807. "I had surmounted many vicissitudes, many anxieties, at the battle of Eylau for instance; and I found myself victorious, dictating laws, having emperors and kings pay me court."

Napoleon was happy at the summit, as top dog. But it proved impossible to stay there.

A mountain climber or commando might recognize some of what drove him. "There is joy in danger," the emperor said.

But why he was so relentlessly driven – by destiny, by character, by genes, by environment, by little red gnomes – remains, in the end, as mysterious as the human heart. Napoleon was the protagonist of his own melodrama, an actor of fate, living out his youthful fantasies on the world stage.

In 1791, at age twenty-two, Napoleon spent six months on an essay called, "What Are the Most Important Truths and Feelings for Men to be Happy?" In it, he denounced ambition and pride.

So much for youthful conviction.

What changed? Ordinary happiness eluded the young man. His father had died when he was a teen. His family had been exiled from Corsica. He was poor, friendless, and awkward. He had no business prospects. His political ambitions on Corsica were dashed. Contentment eluded him, while military opportunity did not. He followed fate, for better and worse.

His afterlife would be fame, he decided. His religious opinion seemed to embrace a vague Deism. "Everything in the world proclaims the existence of God," he said. But he suggested that a logical object of worship would be the sun, and didn't talk of heaven or hell.

"Paradise is a central spot where the souls of all men arrive by different roads," he said once. "Each sect has its own path."

He made the Catholic Church a temporary political ally, but never restored its property or power. "The ignorance of priests is the greatest plague ever inflicted upon the world," he grumbled.

So what did drive his soul?

Napoleon seemed genuinely passionate about Josephine, even though it is doubtful she ever fully loved him. His delirious dying words were, "France, the Army, Head of the Army, Josephine."

That would seem to sum up his priorities.

But while Bonaparte divorced her only with reluctance, married a second time to sire a son, had a string of mistresses, and used sex for emotional release, he lacked any high opinion of women. Reflecting his conservatism, his legal code rolled back some of the feminist gains won in the French Revolution. It made women subordinate to husbands, took away many of their property rights, and made divorce more difficult.

Was Napoleon a misogynist?

It would be more accurate to say he had the prejudices of an old-fashioned eighteenth century warrior. When he said, "Women are nothing but machines for producing children," it was meant in part as provocative insult, and in part as twisted compliment, since he needed reproduction to provide future soldiers.

He could be deliberately rude, criticizing one woman's feet, and another's dress, to their faces. "Women should employ themselves with their knitting needles," he told Madame de Staël, who was arguably his intellectual superior and annoyed him because of it.

More seriously, he believed royalist France had been weakened by a feminine court at Versailles and that military masculinity would produce a stronger society. "Women ruled everything," he complained of society under Louis XVI. And because of that, he said, the king folded before the rabble.

Nonetheless, we wince at pronouncements that would get a supervisor fired in the America of today.

"Girls cannot be better brought up than by their mother, public education does not suit them."

"Women think only of dress and pleasure."

"Female virtue has been held in suspicion from the beginning of the world, and ever will be."

Such commentary was ultimately wasteful, depriving him of the resources and wit of half the human the race. But it was typical of his time.

Similarly, Napoleon reflected the racism of his era. He tried to re-impose slavery in present-day Haiti in 1802, eventually losing an army and his brother-in-law general in the attempt. The war killed thirty thousand French and at least ten times that many Haitians. He made no apologies. "If I were black, I would be for the blacks," he said, "but being white, I am for the whites."

Napoleon was in the end a man with no real romantic partner, no friends outside his professional colleagues and servants, starved of love by his mother, and with disdain for his father and siblings. "I was never in love," he said, "except perhaps with Josephine a little."

He was unwilling to invest in affection. "It takes time to make oneself be loved," he remarked after seizing power. "Even when I had nothing to do I always vaguely felt that I had no time to waste."

Love as a waste? "I believe love to be hurtful to society," he said, "and to the individual happiness of men. I believe, in short, that love does more harm than good." Anyone having experienced the pain of a broken heart or the frustrations of partnership might sympathize. But it is the opposite of the teachings of Jesus, not to mention being at odds with the Beatles!

Napoleon, militant from nature, made a Faustian bargain. He would trade love for renown, and affection for acclaim.

Is Napoleon, then, a model for conduct? We can't argue with his extraordinary success. His climb was almost without equal in history. The isolated boy became the most significant man in the world.

But he doesn't appear to have enjoyed it much. He worked maniacally, sometimes going up to three days straight without sleeping. Napoleon could no more stop striving than stop breathing. Difficulty and challenge were ingredients of his fame. "Misfortunes have their heroism and their glory," he said.

One is reminded of the Greek hero Achilles, who chose glory over long life when given the choice by the gods.

Napoleon was soaring rocket and plunging meteor, done at age forty-five, imprisoned on a lonely island, everything he achieved gone except this: he left the world a profoundly different place. He institutionalized some of the ideals of the French Revolution. He confirmed the political independence of the New World, and remade the map of the Old. He put Europe on its modern course. He became a template for every wily dictator and self-promoting politician who has come since. He was man at his best, and worst.

One suspects he felt the entire trajectory a reasonable bargain.

"Deep tragedy is the school of great men," Napoleon concluded.

Bonaparte succeeded because he imagined what he *could* do, not what he should do or was supposed to do. He mastered luck through work. He didn't give up.

He failed because he couldn't moderate his own aggression. He overreached. He repeated the same formula too many times. His pride left him unable to compromise, and thus unable to achieve lasting peace.

It was quite an arc, with a startlingly remote end: that wave-washed rock of an island, that unmarked grave, that absence of family.

So think carefully what you wish for.

And from Bonaparte's examples, take lesson.

A NAPOLEON TIMELINE

HIS RISE:

August 15, 1769: Born in Ajaccio, Corsica.

1777: France begins support of the American Revolution.

January, 1779: Napoleon learns French at Autun, France.

May 17, 1779: Begins study at the military academy at Brienne.

October 17, 1784: Enrolls in the *Ecole Militaire* in Paris.

February 24, 1785: Napoleon's father Carlo dies.

October 28, 1785: Graduates in artillery from *Ecole Militaire.*

November 3, 1785: Stationed in Valence.

July 14, 1789: Storming of the Bastille and start of the French Revolution.

June 13, 1793: Napoleon and his family flee Corsica for France.

October 9, 1793: Given command of artillery at siege of Toulon.

December 22, 1793: Made brigadier general after Toulon victory.

August 9-20, 1794: Imprisoned as supporter of Robespierre, then released.

October 5, 1795: Crushes royalist mob in Paris with artillery.

October 15, 1795: Meets Josephine at home of Paul Barras.

March 9, 1796: Marries Josephine.

March 11, 1796: Leaves Paris to take command of Army of Italy.

May 10, 1796: Wins battle of Lodi and begins to dream big.

November 17, 1796: Wins the Battle of Arcole.

January 14, 1797: Wins Battle of Rivoli.

October 17, 1797: Completes Italian campaign with Treaty of Campo-Formio.

May 19, 1798: Leaves France on Egyptian campaign.

July 21, 1798: Wins Battle of the Pyramids and occupies Cairo.

August 1, 1798: Admiral Nelson destroys Napoleon's fleet at the Battle of the Nile.

May 20, 1799: Defeated at Acre, in present-day Israel, and begins retreat to Egypt.

August 23, 1799: Leaves Egypt to return to France and seize power.

November 9-10, 1799: Following a *coup d'etat,* Napoleon becomes First Consul.

June 14, 1800: After crossing the Alps, wins battle of Marengo.

July 15, 1801: Signs Concordat ending French schism with Catholic Church.

March 25, 1802: Treaty of Amiens with Britain.

May 1, 1802: Restructures French education.

May 3, 1803: Sells Louisiana Territory to the United States.

December 2, 1804: Napoleon crowns himself Emperor.

March 17, 1805: Napoleon crowned as king of Italy.

October 21, 1805: British victory at Trafalgar ends any chance of invading England.

December 2, 1805: Napoleon defeats Austria and Russia at Austerlitz.

June 14, 1807: Having defeated Prussia in 1806, defeats the Russians at Friedland.

July 7, 1807: Tsar Alexander I makes peace with the Treaty of Tilsit. Arguably the summit of Napoleon's career.

HIS FALL:

November 30, 1807: Beginning of embroilment in Portugal and Spain.

December 15, 1809: Divorces Josephine.

April 2, 1810: Marries Archduchess Marie-Louise of Austria.

June 24, 1812: Invades Russia. By December his army is destroyed.

March 17, 1813: Prussia declares war again on France.

June 21, 1813: The Battle of Vitoria assures British victory in Spain.

October 19, 1813: Napoleon defeated by Russia, Prussia, and Austria at the battle of Leipzig.

March 31, 1814: Paris falls to the Allies.

April 4, 1814: Napoleon abdicates and is soon exiled to Elba.

March 1, 1815: Escapes Elba and again seizes power in France.

June 18, 1815: Defeated at Waterloo.

October 16, 1815: Exiled to St. Helena.

March 5, 1821: Napoleon dies.

SUGGESTED READING

Napoleonic literature is vast. For those interested in reading more about Bonaparte's life, here are some suggestions to get started:

The Horizon Book of the Age of Napoleon, by J. Christopher Herold. (American Heritage Publishing Company, 1963.) While dated, this overview by a National Book Award winner captures the romance, glory, and horror of Bonaparte's era. His dramatic and colorful *Bonaparte in Egypt* inspired my own novel, *Napoleon's Pyramids.*

The Age of Napoleon, by Will and Ariel Durant. (Simon and Schuster, 1975.) Part of their civilization series.

The Age of Napoleon, by Susan P. Conner. (Greenwood Press, 2004.) A concise summary.

Napoleon: A Life, by Andrew Roberts. (Viking, 2014.) The newest and in many ways the best one-volume biography of Bonaparte, enlivened by recently discovered correspondence and the author's travel to key points. Generally favorable to its subject.

Napoleon Bonaparte, by Alan Schom. (HarperCollins, 1997.) This scholarly and incisive biography gives a sharply critical assessment of Napoleon.

Napoleon: A Biography, by Frank McLynn. (Arcade, 1997.) A brisk, highly readable biography that includes the emperor's personal life and a dash of psychoanalysis. McLynn humanizes his subject.

The Rise of Napoleon Bonaparte, and *The Reign of Napoleon Bonaparte*, by Robert Asprey. (Basic Books, 2000 and 2001.) A comprehensive, two-volume biography by a former military man that is judicious in its assessments.

Napoleon for Dummies, by J. David Markham. (Wiley, 2005.) Don't be put off by the title of this concise and insightful work by a Napoleonic scholar; it is a thoughtful and brisk introduction.

Napoleon, *For and Against*, by Pieter Geyl. (Yale University Press, 1949.) A summary of a century and a half of scholarship about Napoleon, and thus a dated but useful guide to the historic literature and conflicting views.

Napoleon, An Intimate Account of the Years of Supremacy, 1800-1814, edited by Proctor Patterson Jones. (Proctor Jones Publishing Company, 1992.) A lavishly illustrated compilation of memoirs by Napoleon's secretary, Meneval, and his valet, Wairy. Gossipy good stuff.

The Bonapartes: The History of a Dynasty, by William H.C. Smith. (Bloomsbury Academic, 2005.) Napoleon's eccentric, greedy, colorful family.

Swords Around A Throne: Napoleon's Grand Armee, by John R. Elting. (Da Capo, 1997.) Elting does a good job of explaining Napoleon's military success. Aimed at military enthusiasts, it is insightful for those readers who will go on to read some of the thousands of books about Napoleon's battles and campaigns.

ABOUT WILLIAM DIETRICH

WILLIAM DIETRICH is the author of twenty-one books of fiction and nonfiction. His New York Times bestselling Ethan Gage series of Napoleonic adventures has sold into thirty-one languages. The author's Pacific Northwest nonfiction won the Pacific Northwest Booksellers Award and the Washington Governor Writers Award. As a career journalist at the *Seattle Times*, Bill share a Pulitzer Prize for coverage of the Exxon Valdez oil spill. Dietrich has been a Nieman Fellow at Harvard University and the recipient of several National Science Foundation journalism fellowships. He lives in Anacortes, WA, USA.

The author's website is www.williamdietrich.com.

Made in the USA
Monee, IL
10 June 2021

70914684R00090